DON'T SAY UM

HOW TO COMMUNICATE EFFECTIVELY
TO LIVE A BETTER LIFE

MICHAEL CHAD HOEPPNER

balance

NEW YORK   BOSTON

Balance

Hachette Book Group
1290 Avenue of the Americas
New York, NY 10104

GCP-Balance.com
@GCPBalance

First Edition: January 2025

Balance is an imprint of Grand Central Publishing.
The Balance name and logo are registered trademarks of Hachette Book Group, Inc.

The publisher is not responsible for websites (or their content) that are not owned by the publisher.

The Hachette Speakers Bureau provides a wide range of authors for speaking events.
To find out more, visit hachettespeakersbureau.com or email HachetteSpeakers@hbgusa.com.

Balance books may be purchased in bulk for business, educational, or promotional use.
For information, please contact your local bookseller or email the Hachette Book Group Special
Markets Department at Special.Markets@hbgusa.com.

Print book interior design by Jeff Stiefel

Library of Congress Cataloging-in-Publication Data

Name: Hoeppner, Michael Chad, author.
Title: Don't say um: how to communicate effectively to live a better life / Michael Chad Hoeppner.
Other titles: Do not say um
Description: First edition. | New York: Balance, 2025.
Identifiers: LCCN 2024016305 | ISBN 9780306834509 (hardcover) |
ISBN 9780306834516 (trade paperback) | ISBN 9780306834523 (ebook)
Subjects: LCSH: Communication—Psychological aspects. |
Interpersonal communication. | Public speaking.
Classification: LCC BF637.C45 H63 2025 | DDC 302.2—dc23/eng/20240804
LC record available at https://lccn.loc.gov/2024016305

ISBNs: 978-0-306-83450-9 (hardcover) 978-0-306-83452-3 (ebook)

Printed in Canada

MRQ-T

1 2024

For Olivia and Bo,
who taught me what being other-focused truly means.

And for my clients.
Your bravery inspires me.
Every day, I ask you to face your fears
and trust that improvement is possible.
And every day you do.

Thank you.

CONTENTS

PART THREE

EVERYTHING YOU NEED TO GET READY, RECOVER, AND RETAIN

PART FOUR
EVERYTHING ELSE

PREFACE

I promise that from this point on I will be a Trustworthy Narrator. Every word you read in this book is one I believe in wholeheartedly and each is intended to help you have a better life.

But...

The first three words you read were a trick. I'm grateful to those first three words—*Don't Say Um*—because they might have caused you to pick up this book and start reading. But they are a trick.

You will learn how to avoid saying *um* in this book, but I never want you to tell yourself, "Don't say *um*," again. In fact, if you have a hardcover edition, I give you full permission to remove the exterior paper jacket and recycle it!

Why on earth, then, did I title this book something that is a doomed direction? Because—very likely—you tell yourself equally doomed directions about speaking all the time: "don't be nervous," "don't be stiff," "don't be salesy," "don't be anxious."

Don't.

Don't.

Don't.

All those phrases have two things in common.

1. They *don't* work.
2. They activate thought suppression.

What is *thought suppression?* You'll learn all about it as we go. For now, just know that I'm not going to ask you to *don't* do anything again.

What will I do?

I will not only help you avoid saying *um*, I will help you be far better at doing the everyday miracle that is talking: that magic trick of turning air into sound, and sound into words. Every time you do that—countless times each day—this book will help you do it better. It won't just help you give a better speech; it will help you live a better life.

But let's not get too ambitious right from the start. Let's begin by exploring a very low-stakes communication situation.

Like running for president of the United States...

(I told you I would be a Trustworthy Narrator; I never said I wouldn't be a sarcastic one.)

Turn the page if you're ready.

INTRODUCTION

HOW TO COMMUNICATE EFFECTIVELY TO LIVE A BETTER LIFE

The stakes for my client could not have been higher. Andrew Yang's 2020 presidential campaign was in danger after a critically panned first debate performance, in which he spoke for the shortest total number of minutes, clocked the fastest speaking speed of any candidate (7.2 words per second), and responded to his first question with a single word: "Sorry?"

The "longest of long shots," according to the *New York Times*, Yang was polling at less than 1 percent, and a second poor performance would doom his candidacy. The Democratic National Committee was striving to narrow the overstuffed presidential field by raising the bar for debate participation with strict fundraising and polling criteria. If he stumbled again, his fundraising would stall and, with that, his campaign.

His team reached out to me: Could I help the candidate turn it around for debate two?

So, he and I spent the next ten days in intensive communication training where I taught him the techniques that I have invented over a decade and a half teaching at institutions like Columbia Business School in the PhD and MBA programs and coaching at organizations like Major League Baseball, World Wildlife Fund, and three of the five biggest law firms in the world.

The night of the debate, I was stationed in his greenroom in Detroit's historic Fox Theatre. My job over for the moment, I had nothing to do but watch CNN like the rest of America. Everyone was tense—a three-hour event might yield as little as five minutes of speaking for a lesser-known candidate like Yang, and regardless of the long-term outcome, he had concepts he desperately wanted to get into the national conversation.

Within minutes of the debate starting, Yang was a different candidate. His message broke through, garnering accolades from major news outlets and top rankings in pundit assessment. Most important of all, that performance course-corrected his campaign: in the next forty-eight hours he had the biggest two-day fundraising total to that point.

I'm proud of the work I did with Andrew. But as proud as I am of that story, it contains a troubling implication—an implication that is directly connected to why I wrote *Don't Say Um.*

The Yang campaign flew me cross-country to join his team within twenty-four hours of his poor debate performance, and then over the course of the next two weeks I was with the candidate virtually round-the-clock.

Here's the troubling implication: What about people who aren't running for president, and who don't have the resources of a presidential campaign? They undoubtedly have important moments in their life when their ability to say words is essential. Do their communication lives count for less?

They can't fly me across the country. But they can read—and use—this book.

This type of training is not just for presidential candidates. It's not just for "presenters." It is for virtually everyone because the subject of this book is *speaking* itself. Talking.

Homo sapiens evolved and outcompeted other hominids in part because of our ability to marshal the firepower of our endlessly complex and flexible language to weave stories, clarify strategies, and make plans to stop the more brawny but less brainy marauders.

Speaking is not a sidecar to being human. It is not a thing we have to do if we want to get a promotion. It is a defining aspect that differentiates us from other life-forms. It is native; it is innate.

It is also completely unavoidable.

Think of the number of daily interactions you have—from the picayune to the profound, the mundane to the monumental. Note how many involve saying words to try to achieve stuff. There are the obvious situations such as delivering a presentation or acing an interview, but consider the following also:

- Raising your hand in class
- Going on a date
- Ensuring your drink order is understood at a crowded coffee shop
- Winning a concession from a customer service representative
- Getting attention for a smart idea
- Negotiating the window of time in which a service provider will deliver assistance
- Communicating clearly in a remote video meeting
- Disputing a claim in a phone call
- Overcoming an objection from a potential customer, political partisan, or reluctant family member
- Making chitchat at a networking event
- Sharing your experience with a loved one during a disagreement

This book will help you with every one of those interactions and more. And it will help by focusing on an unconventional place: delivery.

All spoken communications can be divided into two primary buckets: content and delivery. *Content* is what you say; *delivery* is how you say it. This book is solely concerned with delivery—not only because it matters more (which it does), but also because it is the fastest, most innovative, and most memorable way to improve the content too. When my clients practice the Lego drill or Finger Walking exercises that you will learn in these chapters, for the first time in their lives they are forced to tolerate silence; in that silence their brain enjoys the benefit of the two resources it needs—time and oxygen—and voilà! They choose more useful, accurate, potent words. Those better words boost their confidence, lower their apprehensiveness, make their speech even more precise, and unlock a positive feedback loop.

Speaking is a skill. It can be learned, practiced, and improved. Just like a pianist learning a new fingering for a difficult run of notes or a chef learning how to caramelize a sauce, this book will teach you the how-to of speaking. Think of it like a YouTube DIY webpage, but a page that solves the most frequent communication derailers.

If you say *um* too much, this book will help you eliminate that nonfluency.

If you talk too fast, this book will help you vary your pace.

If your voice quivers when you're nervous, this book will help you speak with resonance and power.

I invented the approach that you're about to learn. It's new. It works. It works fast. And it works forever.

- *It's new.* This book isn't a repackaging of the same old bromides about delivering memorable messages or speaking "authentically." Its unique approach activates embodied cognition, circumvents thought suppression, and can liberate you from years of communication struggles.
- *It works.* The exercises achieve changes that can be measured, not only by experts, but also by anyone with a smartphone or a watch and pad of paper.
- *It works fast.* If you have fifteen minutes to read a chapter and do the included exercises, you can perform measurably better in the subject of said chapter.
- *It works forever.* You won't just remember what you learn because the tools are new and surprising (which they are). But, because of their physical nature, when you learn and practice these exercises they create muscle memory, and the skills stick around for the long haul.

How can I have such confidence in my approach? Because I've witnessed its effectiveness countless times, helping such people as Tim Shriver, chairman of the Special Olympics; Costis Maglaras, dean of Columbia Business School; and Claudia Salomon, the first female president of the International Court of Arbitration. Those are just the people with whom I don't have firstborn-child-claiming NDAs. I could tell you other names, but then I would have to kill you.

The methodology in *Don't Say Um* comes from a decade and a half of helping thousands of people and professionals and watching them succeed where other methods failed. Because no one ever asked them to stack Lego blocks, adhere a line of masking tape to their floor, or throw a Wiffle ball. And by doing the hands-on exercises in this book, you will be able to use dozens of fun drills that will get you out of your head and into your body, where sound actually comes from.

Don't Say Um is structured in four parts.

In Part One, I give the same overview of the issue that I gave my students at Columbia. I first make the argument that public speaking isn't going anywhere and the ability to do it effectively will always be the difference between persuading your listener to hire you, promote you, assign you, or elect you—and not.

But then I deconstruct the very notion of public speaking. There is no such thing; there is simply speaking. And unless it's happening as an inner monologue, it is always public. It's a thing you will probably have to do, every day, each day, for many years to many audiences, and much of your ability to achieve your hopes and dreams is directly linked to how well you do it.

Then I explain that anyone can speak well when it matters by unlocking their own innately powerful communication instrument. Ever notice that babies can create sound about as efficiently as a fire engine? Powerful communication is inborn. After practicing and applying my kinesthetic techniques, you will be able to communicate—in any situation—like the greatest version of you.

Parts Two, Three, and Four build on that foundation. Part Two contains the bulk of the how-tos: You'll get the tools you need to avoid monotone, mumbling, rambling, and—yes—even the word *um*. Part Three offers better approaches to sidestep four frequent pitfalls. You'll learn how to prepare before you speak, how to navigate nerves, how to recover from mistakes, and how to retain what you've learned. Part Four is the briefest. It includes just two chapters, both about what comes next. The first looks at the future of artificial intelligence and its impact on spoken communications; the second looks at the future of you and your impact on the world.

Chapters are structured by both priority and progression. You'll get the most out of this book if you read it start to finish because the skill sets build on one another, but I've written it in such a way that you can use this like a cookbook. Maybe the first time you read a well-loved cookbook you made it through the intro and some of the foundational principles, but soon you got excited and jumped to the Flourless Chocolate Cake. Well, there is a delicious recipe for Flourless Chocolate Cake in this book, and it's called "How to Choose Your Words (and Avoid 'Um')," and if you'd like to taste it, feel free to skip to Chapter 7. Sometimes it's nice to watch the step-by-step instructions for a recipe too, so you'll also have access to videos. You can go to dontsayum.com any time to get how-to demos (led by yours truly) and extra goodies, such as an interactive app.

You should read this whole book from start to finish. Every chapter will help you become a better speaker. But if you're really just interested in learning how to solve a specific challenge, you have my blessing—as the person who spent years writing this—to skip around as much as you like. Whatever makes it most likely that you use this book and these drills—and use them over and over—is the best way to read it.

Because if you use this book, you are going to be surprised at how much you improve, and how fast. My favorite thing about being a coach is watching people who have spent years thinking they are "bad" at speaking suddenly understand that they have just been tripping themselves up by focusing on the wrong solutions. Within a couple of hours, we have undone the bad habits and gotten people on a new path to being the best possible advocate for their own ideas.

The last thing I'll say in this introduction is this:

COMMUNICATION MATTERS,
IT'S MORE PHYSICAL THAN YOU THINK,
AND THERE ARE THINGS YOU CAN DO TO IMPROVE IT.

Let's begin.

PART ONE

EVERYTHING YOU NEED TO KNOW

CHAPTER 1

THIS APPLIES TO EVERYONE

I once helped a sociologist who had just finished her PhD. As an academic, she was a groundbreaking scholar, brilliant thinker, and beloved mentee of several professors.

But she couldn't get a job. And she was becoming panicked. She was considering rethinking her geography, her ambitions, even her career. She felt that people didn't take her seriously and that was evidence her research and writing weren't good enough.

Over a period of four months, I coached her to master three behaviors: (1) rather than speaking at a relentlessly fast speed, we used the kinesthetic drills you will learn in this book to vary pace—one of five musical dynamics of vocal presence; (2) rather than resonating her voice primarily in her sinuses, we used the physical and vocal warm-ups you will learn in this book to unlock resonance throughout the body; (3) rather than littering her language with the useless modifier *like*, we used the linguistic precision exercises you will learn in this book to actively choose words. Note that none of those adjustments had anything to do with her research.

Four months later, she had a job in her chosen field.

Obviously, many factors went into her getting hired, but one of the key ones was her ability to get out of a deeply self-destructive pattern. She was stuck in an unhelpful cycle of beating up on herself and her research, trying harder to improve her research, feeling even worse when people weren't impressed, then trying even harder to improve her research, and so on and so forth without putting any focus on how she was communicating about her research.

I share that story not to show that I'm a miracle worker but rather to show what miracles can come from focusing on delivery for even a fraction of the time we focus on content.

And focusing on delivery doesn't mean focusing on how you're feeling. I founded a communication training company, GK Training, in 2010, and as head of that organization, I have been coaching and teaching in industries that range from pharma to legal to finance to tech to academia to reinsurance to retail ever since. In all those industries and to all those audiences, I tell my clients the same thing:

> I actually don't care how you feel. At all. I hope you feel calm or centered or serene or capable or authoritative because those are all nice feelings, but ultimately I only care that you can come across well no matter how you're feeling: when you're feeling scared or insecure or nervous or self-loathing or unimportant or "like a fraud" or any of the other uncomfortable feelings we humans experience. True confidence in your ability as a communicator comes from knowing that you can perform no matter how you are feeling.

Here's a silly example.

Take 1: You're a boy in high school hanging out with a group of friends trying to choose a movie to watch. You have an idea. You say—very rapidly—in a light, ungrounded voice, "Well, uh, we could, maybe, like, see, like, y'know, *Frozen II*, cuz I heard it's not that, uh, lame, but you know I don't really care or whatever..." and trail off with maybe another word or two that become less and less audible.

Your friends laugh at you. You don't see the movie.

Take 2: You're a boy in high school hanging out with a group of friends trying to choose a movie to watch. You have an idea. You choose your words deliberately and speak in a full, grounded voice using a generous amount of breath: "This is going to sound crazy, but I heard *Frozen II* is really good. Apparently, it explores a darker side of Arendell. Let's see that."

Your friends laugh at you. You may still not see the movie, but you've got a hell of a lot better shot.

If that high school kid who wants to see *Frozen II* came to me—perhaps via his parents, who want to give him a better chance to succeed in life—and said something like "I feel really socially awkward in situations and I don't feel like people listen to me and I never know when I should interject and then when I do interject, I feel like people laugh at me," I would not

+ Ask him why he feels awkward
+ Ask him what he thinks makes him feel so awkward
+ Ask him when this awkwardness started
+ Ask him around whom does this awkwardness happen
+ Ask him any other questions that have the word *awkward* in them

If I tell you, right now, in this very instant:
Don't.
Feel.
Awkward.
…do you feel more or less awkward than you did the split second before you read that command?

Instead, I would teach that high school student

+ How to speak more clearly
+ How to find strength and power in the physical bearing of his body
+ How to use his words precisely
+ How to use vocal variety to gain attention

Note that none of those sentences has the word *awkward* in it.

All those sentences *do* have the word *how* in them. Not *why* or *what*, but *how*. Because the high school student can do something about the how. It's something he can control.

And you can too. And that is the focus of this book.

CHAPTER 2

SHOULDN'T THIS BE EASY? OR...LET'S UNLEARN WHAT YOU'VE LEARNED

Let's start with a contradiction. How is something so easy so hard? We walk through our day-to-day speaking and communicating with people in a variety of situations and on a variety of topics, and much of the time we don't even give it a second thought; it's so natural and comfortable to us. And yet, put us in a high-stakes situation and the simple activity of talking to a person or a group of people can feel like the most challenging, frightening, unnerving, and even insurmountable task we have ever faced.

Most of us can relate to feeling that way, whether the scenario is speaking in public, pitching a product or service, interviewing for a coveted role, negotiating a salary, or something else. What we do flawlessly when we're not thinking about our communication can become utterly painful when we get into situations that make us uncomfortable. For any of these things—public speaking, asking for business, negotiating a salary—you can get better, no matter if you consider this a weakness or a strength.

The skills I'm teaching in this book can be honed and improved for the rest of your life. But they take practice. And I mean practicing the

right stuff: the right drills, the right mindsets, the right habits. This
entire book is built around helping you unlock those. Because people face
a lot of detours, obstacles, and traps. Some are self-imposed, some come
from other people.

So, before we can move in the right direction, we should look at what
we need to avoid at all costs.

If you're reading this book, there is a good chance this is not your first
attempt to improve as a communicator. You may have had multiple rides
on the improve-your-communication merry-go-round. If that's the case, I
can almost certainly promise you that you've been the victim of bad advice
somewhere along the line.

A remarkable amount of the feedback you hear coming out of the
mouths of so-called communication experts is utterly worthless and in
fact less than worthless because it actually makes things worse. How?
Much of the time it's either (1) generalized or (2) negative. Often it's both.
I call this the "General Don't" school of coaching. What do I mean?

1. *General:* "Just be yourself." "Just be confident." "Just have fun."
   Or the worst: "Just relax." If you have received advice starting
   with the word *just,* there is a strong probability it lacked the
   actual tools for *how* you should achieve these "relax, be confident, be yourself" commands. Most of the time it's because
   the advice givers don't know themselves. The feedback is
   completely general and unactionable.

2. *Negative:* You will also hear perfectly well-meaning people give utterly unhelpful advice that starts with *don't.* You
   may already have a tired old tape playing in your head that
   repeats one of these mantras: "Don't fidget." "Don't click your
   pen." "Don't jangle the change in your pocket when you're in
   front of the room." "Don't fold your arms." "Don't keep your
   arms behind your back." "Don't move your hands too much."
   "Don't keep your hands frozen." I challenge you to read that
   last string of phrases and have the least idea of what you
   should do with your hands. If you wanted to sabotage someone before a big speech, you would be wise to generously help

them with the following advice: "In today's speech try not to say *um* so much; it undermines your credibility." Then sit back and watch the number of *ums* they say explode.

Think of someone you know who has a bad communication habit. Perhaps they talk a mile a minute. When someone suggests, "Don't talk so fast," does that person ever respond, "Wow—I have never ever heard that before. Thanks for telling me. I'll absolutely slow down now"? *No!* Typically, bad communication habits do not result from lack of awareness; they result from lack of know-how.

THOUGHT SUPPRESSION (OR HOW NOT TO SUCCEED)

This brings us to thought suppression, which is the reason why all those *don'ts* don't work.

If I say to you right now, "Don't think about...
...a *sunflower*."

Were you successful?

Likely not. Because we were just trafficking in thought suppression. A colleague of mine at Columbia, Dr. Adam Galinksy, studies this, and it turns out humans are lousy at thought suppression. It's the pink elephant trick, and it's not your fault. If you point out a rock to a bicyclist and tell them, "Don't hit that rock!" are they more or less likely to hit the rock?

You guessed it, you genius you! The bicyclist is more likely.

So now you understand the preface and why the title of this book is a trick: the instruction *Don't Say Um* is in fact an example of thought suppression!

Avoiding *um* is a valid goal—valid enough that I dedicate an entire chapter, Chapter 7, to the topic of reducing filler language and we dive into what I call *linguistic precision*. But the way to reduce that filler is not thought suppression. In fact, that's the worst thing for it.

Thought suppression is so challenging because of a principle called *distinction*, which I learned about from Professor Derek Cabrera at Ithaca College.

Distinction is the act of categorizing things by given criteria. Our brains are excellent at this. We do this constantly; we distinguish between things and put them into groups. This ability allows us to separate the edible seeds from the poisonous ones and accomplish every other act of distinguishing we need to do to create a society and survive as a species.

Let's practice distinction right now. I want you to do a quick pen-and-paper activity (or you can even use your finger as an imaginary pencil). Please circle all the *x*'s in the following lines:

T H I O F O I I F K B L O H I Y G J
K B K B J G U Y Z F J V K J L O J P I G Y V J H V Z Z
X X X F I K U G W E U V X X

Now go back and circle all the *y*'s.

Once you're done with that, circle all the *z*'s.

What you have just done is distinguish *x*'s, then *y*'s, and then *z*'s from all the other letters in that block of text. Likely, you did it so well that even as you were finishing up the *y*'s your brain also began to note the location of the z's because it had figured out the pattern of looking for consecutive letters in the alphabet. In that moment, your brain was dividing life into two categories: the letter x, and everything else in the known universe. So when you tell your brain, "Don't think about x," it is required to think about it and compare it—in all its complete and fulsome x-ness—to any other non-x thing anywhere in the past, present, and future.

Distinction, in fact, puts whatever pink elephant you're trying not to think about on one side of a scale and the rest of the known universe on the other side. You have made the two equivalent, and your brain is virtually obligated to think about the pink elephant—obsessively.

You can experience thought suppression in other everyday ways too. For example, anyone who has ever tried meditation is aware of how futile thought suppression is. It's why the first lesson of meditation is to begin to get comfortable with simply noticing your thoughts rather than trying to make the unproductive ones—like "I can't meditate!" or "What about all the emails I have to answer?"—go away.

Another way to examine thought suppression is to consider "the imp of the perverse," the popular psychology term for the tendency that humans have to fixate on wholly inappropriate, probably illegal, at times pathological, and definitely diabolical things, for the simple reason that we know we shouldn't do them. If you've ever been aware of the strange temptation to drop an object off a skyscraper, throw something at a live actor onstage, yell "Fire!" in a movie theater, or some other totally awful, reprehensible act, you are acquainted with the imp of the perverse. The fact that you were able to avoid doing what the imp said—but unable to stop thinking about it—shows the power and futility of thought suppression.

So, instead of all those other *don'ts* you may have heard or been told about, I'll give you a new *don't* to repeat in your head instead:

DON'T LISTEN TO ANYONE WHO STARTS OFF THEIR COMMUNICATION TEACHING BY SAYING, "DON'T..."

SELF-HELP (ALSO, NOT!)

But it's not just the unhelpful coaching we get from others that can inadvertently undermine us. We mess ourselves up, too, in a variety of ways. Here are four of the most common I see with clients.

"I Just Want to Be Natural"

When I ask my clients—from people just entering the workforce to C-suite execs managing billion-dollar companies—to experiment with speaking a little louder or a little slower or standing a little taller or moving a little more freely, inevitably they reply: "This doesn't feel natural." Of course, the remark has nothing to do with what is truly natural to humans and everything to do with what is habitual to that individual. One CEO I worked with who had terrible posture gave me that objection when I had him standing just a bit more upright. Six months later, I got a hearty thank-you from him and his chiropractor.

Many of the things we think of as natural to how we communicate and carry ourselves are simply habitual. And improving as a communicator depends on you freeing yourself up to have a slightly larger idea of who you are and how you can be in any given situation. If you don't buy this yet, let me ask you a question. If you are in a room with a two-year-old who is playing, running, and laughing and a twenty-year-old doing the same things, which one seems more "natural" and "authentic"? What about the two- and twenty-year-old versions of yourself? Which one was more "authentic"? Which one had a wider range of communication? Which one was more compelling to watch? Which one was more captivating? If your answer is "the twenty-year-old version," congratulations...you're in the extreme minority. If you answered the other way, congratulations also...you're in good company with the rest of us.

We accrue habits over time as we rein ourselves in, layer on artifice, build in defense mechanisms, limit our exposure, and collect all the other adaptations we make on the trying journey to adulthood. But your ability to be a skilled, powerful, and flexible communicator is directly tied to your ability to be more, not less. So, I'm going to ask you to loosen up ever so slightly the notion of what is natural and authentic for you.

As one immediate test to this . . . *Freeze! Don't move a muscle!* Stay precisely in the position you are in. Now ask yourself, "Is this my 'natural' posture?" Very likely you're slouched over, crisscrossed, or corkscrewed in some postural position that has little to do with "natural" posture. It has much more to do with habit and gravity.

"I Don't Want to Overprepare"

I hear "I don't want to overprepare" a lot as well. Inevitably, it's coming from someone who is so far from ever coming across as overprepared that I have a hard time knowing whether they're being sarcastic. From years of helping people communicate better, I have learned that fear of "overpreparation" or of being "overly polished" is usually a defense mechanism masking one of these two truths:

1. I'm embarrassed to practice out loud (in front of anyone—even myself!).
2. I don't feel like taking the time to work on this, so I'll just wing it instead and tell myself I'm better when I wing things.

Think of a story that you have told dozens of times: Maybe it's an embarrassing anecdote; maybe it's a favorite joke. I bet there are portions that you tell the same way every time. But the success of that story or joke depends on you telling it anew with just as much freshness, drama, and suspense as the very first time. You would never say about a joke, "I overprepared—I've told this joke before." Most of the time, lack of authenticity or freshness comes from lack of commitment, not overpreparation.

The risks from being underprepared and unpracticed far, far outweigh the risks from being overprepared. And if you happen to be in the minority of people who really, truly do overprepare, it's likely not because of "over" preparing but rather *how* you're preparing. Which leads me to the third way we create our own obstacles to improving.

We Memorize Our Mistakes

Anyone who has ever had to undo a bad sports coach's "help" understands this principle: If you keep practicing the same mistake, your muscles perfect how to make that mistake. Your muscles literally memorize the mistake. Speaking is the same way. I once worked with an executive who claimed he couldn't memorize—even a couple of sentences. So I asked him to demonstrate this and deliver a speech to me that he had given recently. He started with his eyes glued to the text of his speech and began reading word for word. Then I asked him to try without reading. He said the first two sentences flawlessly, but then after the first part of the third sentence, he went blank, turned beet red, cursed at himself, and yelled at me: "See?!" I asked him (politely) to try it again. He did the exact same thing, down to the precise word where he went blank. He said, "See! I can't memorize anything! I worked and worked and worked on this speech. I'm just not someone who can memorize!" He was getting infuriated—not at me, but at himself. I asked him (even more gently) to try it one more time. Same exact results.

None of this surprised me. Most of us can memorize things. We memorized dozens of phone numbers before cell phones made it less essential. We memorize addresses, recipes, the beginnings of TV shows. We memorize the lyrics to songs—even ones we hate. This executive's problem was not that he couldn't memorize; he had actually memorized his speech too well! He had—flawlessly and perfectly—memorized reciting the first few sentences in his head; getting to the part where he forgot what was next; berating himself for being stupid, slow, and forgetful; and then continuing the speech from that point forward. I have no idea how many times he practiced that way before we met. I imagine it was a lot.

So, we worked to pry some of his muscle memory free from that habit. The first step was noticing where he had written that section on the page. The word he kept forgetting was right after the end of a line on the

page, not at the end of a sentence—which told me that he had been trying to memorize each line on the page rather than the complete thought.
Likely, he had been looking at the page, practicing one line, then the next,
then the next—memorizing random collections of words that had been
divided and grouped solely on the basis of font style and size and by how
the word-processing software had distributed them on the page. When
it came time to recite the whole page, his brain and body hadn't learned
the connective tissue in between each line. Once he understood how that
pattern started, we were able to work past that one section of the speech.
Much to his amazement, he could then deliver whole sections of the
speech flawlessly without notes.

This is not to say that speeches even need to be memorized! In fact,
it's rare that an entire speech must be memorized word for word. But I
bring it up as an example of how practicing in an unhelpful way can do
more harm than good.

We Don't Practice Out Loud

If you were trying to improve your athletic ability, would you prepare only
by looking at some visual aids that show the angle of a good swing? If
you were trying to change your running stride, would you prepare only
by writing down the distance of your step and strike pattern? If you were
trying to master the violin, would you prepare only by writing down the
notes you were about to play?

Likely no.

Yet we make this basic mistake all the time when it comes to speaking. I work with smart, decisive, efficient executives who have "prepared"
for a speaking event by drafting, redrafting, revising, and re-revising their
words or visual aids and not actually speaking them out loud a single
time. These are people who would never dream of rolling out an untested
product. Yet when it comes to speaking, they expect themselves to be able
to speak brilliantly after spending 100 percent of their time writing and
0 percent speaking. Oral communication is a physical art. Becoming a
better speaker takes muscle prep and practice. It's more akin to preparing
for an athletic event than it is cerebral strategizing.

So, if these are some of the ways we get screwed up as communicators—both listening to the unhelpful suggestions of others and ourselves—what is a better way?

The first thing we have to do is define what good looks like. And that's how we'll start the next chapter.

16

CHAPTER 3

THREE THINGS YOU DIDN'T
KNOW YOU KNEW

To start identifying what we're going for, let's agree on a definition.
What the heck is *great communication?*

Really. What is it?

I have a definition that might come as a surprise: Great communication is you when you are at your most other-focused. What do I mean?

Counterintuitively, your communication is at its very best when
you're not thinking about *your communication*. It's best when you are not
thinking about yourself at all. It's best when you are keenly and earnestly
focused on helping someone else.

Try this thought experiment: Your dearest friend in the whole world
comes to you in crisis. Imagine whatever truly dire circumstances you
like. They have committed a crime, are considering leaving their spouse,
have been fired, have received a diagnosis. We're going to come back to
this thought experiment over and over, so I want you to get someone specific in mind. In fact, to make this as vivid as possible, please write in the
initials of that person.

My friend's initials: _____

My friend's most likely crisis: _____

_____

See yourself in that conversation. Visualize how you are sitting, speaking, listening…and I want you to consider:

+ Is your eye contact direct and sustained?
+ Does your voice have variety and dynamic range?
+ Are your gestures free, fluid, and specific?
+ Are you using sufficient breath to create sound?
+ Are you speaking deliberately enough that you can choose the words you want to say?
+ Are you enunciating those words clearly enough to be understood?

The answer, of course, to all those questions is an emphatic yes. Because you would be doing all those things for the simple, profound purpose of understanding and being understood.

Communication is not arbitrary. We don't use powerful communication tactics like gestures and vocal variety and eye contact because they convey presence and gravitas. We use them because, as animals, we have evolved to affect one another socially, vocally, and physically. You are already an exceptional communicator—when you are utterly focused on reaching someone else.

SURPRISE 1

<u>Great communication *comes from being focused on the other person.*</u> Everyone knows that in a sale or in a negotiation or on a date, your success depends on how much you can reach the other person. Although you may know this, do you do it? Think in terms of eye contact for a moment. Attendees in training workshops often challenge me about this point by saying something like "too much" eye contact is

+ Awkward
+ Forced
+ Strange
+ Uncomfortable
+ Confrontational

And yet, if I asked any of those people to accomplish the following task, their eye contact would automatically be sustained, steady, focused—flawless: A three-year-old comes running to you sobbing about a minor injury they just suffered. Figure out what happened.

Our eye contact in that situation is instantly perfect because all our senses are marshaled to get as much information as quickly as possible from our audience (in this case, a crying child).

I realize the "surprise" of other-focus may sound absurdly obvious. But, as an example, I frequently work with people who are so mixed up and self-conscious about what to do with their hands they could practically declare, "I have these hands that showed up on my arms that belong to someone else and I have no idea where I should put them! What should I do?" Upward of 90 percent of the people I coach on public speaking will ask some form of that question! And yet, very few of those same people would ask me, "When I'm out to dinner with my friends, what should I do with my hands?" At dinner, people are focused on (1) *their* friends, and (2) *their* food. In public speaking, their focus is on (1) *my* hands, and (2) *my* nerves.

The reason they don't know what to do with their hands when giving a speech is that their focus is not where it should be. They are not focused on the audience. They are entirely focused on "What do I do with the alien things hanging off the ends of my wrists?!"

They're not self-centered though. If you ask these people who the most important person is in any given communication situation, you or the client, you or the audience, you or your team, they all know the right answer—the second one in each of those options. But because of how they've been trained and taught, when they begin to speak, the most important person in the room instantly becomes themselves.

SURPRISE 2

The second surprise follows along from the first: *great communication comes from using more of ourselves, not less.*

When we're other-focused, we tend to use more of ourselves: more gestures, more vocal variety, more breath, more eye contact. Great communicators speak in a low and even voice. They also speak in a high and light one at times. They speak fast and slow, loud and soft. They use all of themselves because they'll do whatever they need to reach their audience. *Vocal variety*—which we'll break down into component parts in Chapter 9—is the term for the dynamic sound mixture we use in our voices to convey difference in meaning and tone. It comes from a deep, organic human need to put a series of grunts and groans together in a melodic, structured, but varied way to let another human know something important, like the location of the bison carcass, the route to the winter feeding grounds, or the best berries to harvest.

Leaders don't speak in low, even voices because someone somewhere identified that people who speak like that are serious and confident; leaders speak like that because they need to convey a specific message to an audience (even an audience of one), and in that moment their organic human communication instrument identified that this particular audience needs to be spoken to in this way *in order for them to understand*.

To prove this point to you further, please answer the following question: Who are the best communicators in the world? (No, really. Who do you think? In fact, write it in here. I'll wait.)

_____

_____

_____

_____

_____

_____

To see my answer, turn the page.

Kids.

Ever lost an argument to a three-year-old? An eye contact battle with a five-year-old? A negotiation with a six-year-old? How much of themselves do they use to get a second cookie, a later bedtime, or access to your phone? All of themselves.

And they don't just use all of themselves in big dramatic ways. Kids use a huge range to communicate even when they're playing or speaking in a gentle or quiet way. Think of one coming over to your ear to tell you a secret they don't want a brother or sister to hear.

As we become adults, we use less of ourselves for a whole myriad of reasons. Boys, particularly during puberty, may try to force their voices down into a lower register to be considered more grown-up. Women may try to neutralize their voices and speak in a steadier, "less emotional" tone to fit in at the workplace.

These adjustments have physical costs. Just one example: We actually lose the ability to use our voices like we used to. If you challenged a six-month-old to a screaming contest, whose voice would give out first? Children can scream all night long and still wake up with a voice. If a typical adult tried that, they would be completely hoarse. And soon they would begin to develop nodes, which are essentially like calluses or blisters on the vocal cords.

Most of the muscles and functions of a healthy adult are more powerful than an infant's by an order of magnitude. Yet—except for singers, actors, and artists who train theirs—the typical adult's voice is far weaker than the infant's.

So, that's the second surprise—good communication *comes from using more of ourselves, not less.* That might seem fairly straightforward. But if I had a nickel for every time I've heard about so-called communication coaching that directs people toward a "more professional style" that is ultimately just more limited, I would have a plethora of nickels.

SURPRISE 3

When a company hires me to work with one of their employees, the first thing they say is, "They just need to be more confident." When an individual comes to work with me, the first thing they say is, "I just want to feel more confident." When a parent hires me to work with their child, the first thing they say is, "I just want to give them more confidence."

Remember the aspiring sociology professor you met in the first paragraph of Chapter 1? I never coached her to "feel more confident." I did give her simple, doable, repeatable actions that improved her presence and delivery.

So, starting now, when it comes to the category of spoken communication, I want you to release any notion, hope, goal, idea, intention, focus, dream, or assumption about confidence. It's a useless place to put our attention.

Because surprise 3 is . . . *you do not need to feel confident in order to project confidence.*

I once worked with a terribly anxious and insecure person in a marketing firm. We'll call him Jim. His company very much wanted to promote him to a leadership role. He was highly responsible, always early and under budget, utterly reliable, and clients loved him once they got to know him. But the company couldn't put him on accounts solo or even feature him in first-time meetings because his delivery, demeanor, and manner were so timid and awkward that they conveyed ineptitude. His manager hoped that, through coaching, he could "be more confident."

On minute one of hour one of day one—despite what his manager had instructed me—I told Jim, "I have no interest in helping you feel more confident. None whatsoever." Once he got over his general shock at this seemingly counterintuitive statement from the person who had been hired to make him more confident in front of potential clients, we were able to proceed with our work. The primary discovery was remarkably simple: we created a regimen that was built around him practicing speaking with a slice of cork held between his front teeth.

You may have heard of historical examples of this basic principle. The most famous is of the ancient Greek orator Demosthenes, who, to overcome weak speaking habits as a child, practiced oration by the seashore. He would fill his cheeks with pebbles and then practice speaking past the dual impediments of the pebbles in his cheeks and the roar of the crashing waves. The cork tool is a version of that same principle, one I learned from a brilliant voice and speech teacher named Andrew Wade, who was the head of voice and speech for the Royal Shakespeare Company.

What we discovered was that Jim had such anxiety about sharing his ideas, his voice, and his thoughts in selling situations that he would subtly but unmistakably shrink. He would actually open his mouth less wide, droop his eyes, collapse his posture, and make various other micro physical adjustments that on a very basic level were about disappearing.

As you learned from our thought-suppression discussion, if I told Jim, "Don't worry, just be confident," his focus would have been precisely where I didn't want it: himself and how not confident he is.

It's not so useful.

What was useful, in this case, was popping a cork between his teeth and making him speak clearly and forcefully enough to be understood—even with that impediment. This technique bypasses the cycle of self-judgment and criticism. It's not about feeling confident or not confident and it's definitely not about why you aren't more confident. It is about a very specific measurement: Can I understand what you're saying even though you have a cork in your mouth? If yes, great! If not, you need to use your lips, mouth, tongue, jaw, and lungs more to help me understand you.

Look at the shift here. Instead of being focused on feelings or thoughts, the focus is physical: Navigate around this impediment and do whatever needs to be done to speak clearly. Instead of the focus being on the self ("be more confident"), the focus is on the audience: Can this person understand what I'm saying? That is the ultimate barometer of good communication.

But how can you shift this new knowledge into action? To unleash how you behave when you are at your most other-focused, you need to learn actionable behavioral tools that unlock a virtuous cycle and tap into your native communication strengths. Said another way, focus on specific things you can *do* instead of vague instructions, self-critical thoughts, or negative feelings. So, instead of a maxim like "Just be yourself," try, "Use the same level of freedom with gestures you use when talking to a friend."

Instead of "Don't be nervous," let's try, "Breathe diaphragmatically so you feel the ribs of your lower back gently pressing against your chair when you inhale."

Instead of "Command the room," let's try, "Enunciate tip-of-tongue consonants (*t, d, n, l*) with as much precision as possible."

By themselves, however, these instructions—though far more specific and actionable—are still insufficient. They are mental instructions for what is ultimately a physical activity—speaking. To unlock the power of these tactics, I coach people around the world to use *embodied cognition* to build positive muscle memory.

What the heck is embodied cognition? That and much more are explained next.

CHAPTER 4

THE VIRTUOUS CYCLE AND WHY YOUR BODY IS THE BEST PLACE TO START

Have you ever tried speaking like a ventriloquist? You know, speaking audible words but endeavoring to hide any physical indication that you're doing so? I want you to do your best impression of a ventriloquist, but a monotonous ventriloquist. Say these words with as little inflection, energy, and adamance as you can, and try to hide from the world the fact that you're even speaking: "Content and delivery."

Thank you for indulging me.

I want you to say those words again, but this time accompanied by a gesture. In a moment when you say *content*, put your left hand in the air and cup your fingers as though they were one half of a binoculars. Your left hand will be held aloft in front of your face and shaped something like this:

Do this as emphatically as you can—completely unlike a monotonous ventriloquist. Use all the vocal emphasis you possibly can while punctuating the word with your gesture. Loud and proud! Go!

Now do the same thing, but with the word *delivery*. This time, put your right hand in a similar position as your left, held aloft in front of your face, shaped roughly like this:

When you say *delivery*, be the opposite of a monotonous ventriloquist again, and use all the emphasis you possibly can. Ready, go!

That activity wasn't just to resurface a long-buried dream of being a famous ventriloquist. Hopefully, it made you consider afresh the two giant buckets of communication I oh-so-briefly introduced earlier. *Content* is what you say—it is your actual words; *delivery* is how you say it—it is everything else: eye contact, tone of voice, gestures, and so forth. You can also probably guess the answer to this next question.

Which matters more?

Feel free to circle your guess.

CONTENT AND DELIVERY

Likely, you circled delivery (the primary subject of this book). You might have circled it even if we hadn't started this chapter with the binoculars-hands activity (and even if I hadn't hinted at the answer in the introduction). Virtually every study ever done examining these two factors concludes that how you say it matters more than what you say. But hopefully that exercise helped you not just know that reality but also feel it.

Actually, I'm not at all interested in which matters more, content or delivery; I'm interested in helping you improve your communication in both by tapping into a virtuous cycle that connects the two divisions, starting with delivery.

Content and delivery reinforce each other, and that reinforcement can trigger a positive or negative feedback loop—the Virtuous (or Vicious) Cycle of Good (or Bad) Communication. Everyone knows that to be true—from content *to* delivery. If you really know your subject matter, you'll deliver it better. Duh. Likewise, if you are unprepared or beyond your depth, you'll likely deliver it less effectively.

But what not everyone knows is this: If you just focus on delivering better, not only will the words sound better when they come out of your mouth, but you'll also actually think of smarter words to say. For example, if a speaker pauses and breathes, not only will the voice sound better when speaking next, but the pause buys the speaker time to think of a better next thing to say. It feels good to have better stuff to say, so it's easier to maintain eye contact. When one maintains eye contact, one can see how the audience is digesting a message, and so one has the opportunity to shape the message on the basis of that audience response. When one shapes the message more, one has a clearer idea of which words are affecting the audience the most and one emphasizes those more. To emphasize words, one needs more breath, and so one breathes in again and the positive cycle continues.

Importantly, note that the previous description of that cycle didn't start by saying "identify what you most want to say" or "begin with a story."

When this cycle doesn't happen, we get what I call the Vicious Cycle of Bad Communication. The speaker is nervous and wants to get through the event as quickly as possible. To get done faster, they speak very quickly. When one speaks quickly with no pauses, one forgets to breathe. When one forgets to breathe, the voice can't be as strong and varied, and it becomes monotone. Monotone voices don't engage an audience as much, so the audience stares blankly back at the speaker with no reaction. The speaker sees bored expressions on the audience's faces, and that confirms their perception that this is painful for all involved, and they redouble their effort to speak even more quickly to get done as soon as possible and prevent boring more people. And when one speaks quickly with no breath, one is more likely to say dumb stuff, and the content gets worse.

The simple kinesthetic activity we did to start the chapter can help you remember content and delivery—as well as the virtuous and vicious cycles that connect them—for the rest of your life. Let's do the activity again. This time hold both hands up in front of your face, cupping them as though you're holding a pair of imaginary binoculars. Note that your left hand looks like the letter C, and your right hand looks like the outer half of a capital D. Sneaky, right?

Now if you keep your hands in those shapes and simply bring your fingertips together, you will see that your hands create an oval—an oval that connects the *c* of content and *d* of delivery. So your hands can remind you of the initial letters of these two divisions and be a visual to symbolize their reinforcing nature.

We can examine a real-world example of this in the case of Jim, the somewhat timid marketing executive you met last chapter. I didn't tell him to say smart things. I just asked him to fight past the impediment of the cork. To do that, Jim had to open his mouth and use his lips more; when he opened his mouth and used his lips more, his brow lifted; when his brow lifted, he appeared more positive; when he appeared more positive, his audience gave him more positive nonverbal feedback; when his audience gave him more positive nonverbal feedback, he could see which messages were resonating, and he adjusted his content accordingly; when he adjusted his content, he was more inclined to make eye contact to see the nods and expressions he was eliciting; when he was more inclined to make eye contact, he was more inclined to unlock his hands and gesture toward the people looking at him; and when he was more inclined to open his hands, he was more inclined to open his mouth more too, and the positive loop began again.

We can all relate to both cycles. What I'm offering you is a tool kit to drive that cycle in a virtuous direction—no matter how you're feeling on a given day or how well you know the subject matter—by focusing on delivery first and letting content take a back seat.

Several traps arise when we try to unlock the virtuous cycle by starting with content. One of them is truly discouraging. Taken to its logical conclusion, if the cycle must start with content, the speaker can only communicate capably after weeks, months, or even years of subject matter mastery. In life, you'll inevitably have to speak with less preparation than you'd like and less expertise than is ideal. Hence the discouraging fallacy at the heart of the content-first approach: You will probably never be enough of a subject matter expert to speak in all the situations you must. It's a fallacy because you can speak well, even if you're not the world's foremost SME—but you need to develop your delivery skills!

But to go further—what if you were that world-renowned subject matter expert? What if you were an absolute savant in your content? Here's my tough-love answer to that *if*: You'd probably be a very similar speaker to the one you are right now. People too often cling to the belief that if they think of smart stuff, then they'll say smart stuff. But, much of the time, this simply isn't accurate. People who are remarkable subject matter experts flub speaking opportunities all the time. People who have authored studies that no one else in the world understands as intimately as they do mess up at the podium.

Another content-first trap is this. Ask yourself this question, and be devastatingly honest with yourself: The last time you performed worse than you would have liked in a speaking situation, was it really because you didn't know enough about the subject, couldn't think of the best phrasing, didn't have enough expertise, or any of the other self-critical claims we make about our communication...or did you just mess up the delivery? Did you talk too fast? Did your voice shake? Did you mumble? Did you stammer? Did you ramble on without sufficient breath?

Having all the brilliant content in the world may never—never—give you the panacea you're seeking.

So, if the content-first approach has limitations, the obvious next question is, How do you improve your delivery and trigger that virtuous cycle? It's time to get physical.

MAKE IT PHYSICAL

I'm going to ask you to work physically—a lot. Because...

1. Communication Is a Physical Art

Speaking is actually closer to an athletic event than a decision-tree flow-chart of ideas. Consider a fun and intriguing phrase I learned from Ralph Zito, an excellent voice and speech teacher who taught at the Juilliard School for many years: "Your voice is your body."

What does that mean? How you alter the physical structure of your human communication instrument—your body—dictates the sounds that you make. Want proof? Plug your nose right now, and then say, "Your voice is your body." Hear how the sound changed? That's because you altered the physical architecture of your body. Try it again, but this time instead of plugging your nose, gently pound on your chest with your fists like a gorilla. Note how your voice registers each of those chest thumps. If you want to speak powerfully, you must get physically engaged.

If you examine how humans create spoken words, it's a tremendously physical activity. The diaphragm drops down, the lungs fill with air, the exhaled air flows over the vocal cords, those cords vibrate and create sound, that sound is amplified throughout all the hollow chambers of the body, then the soft palate, tongue, cheeks, and lips all move in remark-able coordination to enunciate, the eyes focus on the listener to look for comprehension, and the hands gesture to emphasize points. Speaking is practically dancing.

Because of the highly physical nature of spoken communications, what I call mental adjustments aren't helpful for improving physical activi-ties. People may have given you very useful advice or suggestions. "Take a deep breath" is an example. But unless they took the time to coach you through what kind of deep breath or you took some moments to focus solely on diaphragmatic breathing, that instruction likely went in one ear and out the other.

2. Being Physical Is Healthier

This second reason can be stated in one sentence. Sitting all day long is bad for your body. Next reason!

3. Being Physical Builds Muscle Memory

You will remember all the tools and lessons in this book better if you use your body. And just like riding a bicycle, once you learn them you will never forget, because you will have built muscle memory. We all know the term *muscle memory*, but let's remind ourselves how powerfully it works. I want you to take out your cell phone. Please go to the number pad screen. Now try to type in a phone number you know very well, but you must do it backward. Please go ahead.

Notice how odd that feels for your fingers? They have physically memorized one pathway, and now you're asking them to go against their muscle memory and do a very different behavior. That's the power of muscle memory.

But the most important reason to make speech physical is . . .

4. Being Physical Activates Kinesthetic Learning and Embodied Cognition

Kinesthetic learning is ultimately learning by doing. *Embodied cognition* is related. It is a fancy name for learning and thinking using your body, not only your brain. Both those terms sound quite complex, but what they mean is very straightforward: use your body as a learning vehicle.

KINESTHETIC TOOLS IN ACTION

Over the last fifteen years working with professionals, executives, and people just like you around the world, I have developed a whole suite of kinesthetic learning tools to drive communication in the virtuous cycle and arrest the fall if it's tending toward a vicious one.

And now that we have laid the foundational principles about good communication, thought suppression, and the virtuous cycle, we can move on to Part Two. I hope the last four chapters have given you some knowledge to think differently; now let's do differently.

PART TWO

———

EVERYTHING YOU NEED TO DO

CHAPTER 5

INTRODUCTION TO YOUR HOW-TO

You have now reached the equivalent of a YouTube DIY page. In the following two sections of *Don't Say Um*, it is my hope that you will find the most practical and innovative tools you have ever encountered for improving as a communicator. Bold hope, I know. But because I encourage people to use transparency powerfully, that is the God's honest truth. The tools and exercises you're about to use are unique in the world of communication training.

+ They're new, but also old (most came from my brain, but one goes back to the ancient Greeks).
+ They're portable (you can do them anywhere).
+ They're modifiable (you can use different props and adjust versions).
+ They're fast (five minutes of doing them is useful).
+ They're versatile enough to be made imperceptible (so you can do them without others knowing!).
+ They work (no parenthetical comment needed).

But most of all, they're easily doable. And once you learn them, they're yours for life.

YOUR BASELINE

To use these next chapters well, we first need to establish a baseline. This brings us to the very first step in the process: Are you aware? By that I mean the first step of improving as a communicator is of course figuring out what needs to be improved. Most people can place themselves in one of these three buckets:

1. You are already aware. This means you are (perhaps even painfully) aware of what your unhelpful communication habits are. Fast talkers, for example, often already know that they are fast talkers.
2. You are aware, but of an inaccurate thing. Many people have a totally erroneous idea of what their challenges are. (The most frequent one I hear is that people believe they "talk with their hands too much.")
3. You are not aware. Some people don't have any sense of which communication challenges are holding them back. This is not a bad place to be, by the way. In some ways, it's easier to begin here, because you may not have spent any time counterproductively trying to implement useless feedback or thought suppression.

If you are in the first category ("You are already aware"), bonus! You get to skip the rest of this chapter. Exult in the glorious feeling! Do not pass Go, do not collect $200, advance directly to Chapter 6. (Or better yet, read the rest of this chapter, too, because you'll learn about other cool stuff like our app and supplemental videos to support your communication journey.)

If you're in the second or third category, the obvious question is, How do you become accurately aware?

You are carrying a powerful tool in your pocket that can help you become far more aware of your communication challenges right now.

It's your smartphone, of course.

Let's talk about what else your phone can do besides absorb every ounce of your attention at all times.

It can also film you.

Reading that, you may have had a sinking feeling in your stomach as you think, "Alright, Michael Chad Hoeppner, you've made me do a few odd things already, but filming myself is a bridge too far." I get that; a lot of people feel that way. Let me tell you why I think you should reconsider.

Look at this equation:

$$P \neq R$$

It stands for "perception does not equal reality." Here's an example: When speakers in high-consequence situations forget what they're saying and "go blank," when asked later how long that moment lasted, they might be off by ten times, thinking one second lasted ten. Filming yourself is a fast, private, and incontrovertible way to see if you're doing what in fact you think you are doing.

Twenty years ago, corporate training programs would charge clients dearly for the experience of getting filmed so that they could see the evidence. Smartphones have made that resource free!

Video gives you the opportunity to examine your verbal presence in isolation (by only listening to the audio) or your physical presence in isolation (by watching without sound).

Last, you can comfort yourself with the thought that by videoing and watching yourself, you are in fact keeping up with the times. For better or worse, social media and smart devices have made filming and watching ourselves a commonplace activity. And if you are more comfortable turning the camera on yourself, consider this: this is not only your opportunity to document memorable moments or post video for others to see but also a chance to use video as a teacher and a gift to yourself.

Convinced? Great! Slightly nervous? Also great! To whatever degree the activities and exercises in this book trigger nerves or butterflies, I challenge you to not only embrace that dynamic but also even cultivate a sense of gratitude about it. This book is a failure-encouraged zone; there are no consequences to performing badly here. Know that the more you encounter and navigate your nerves or anxieties or apprehensions here, the more practice and experience you'll have doing it for "out there," where your performance does matter.

So now I'd like you to film yourself—two times. If this feels like a risk, thank you for taking a risk with me. If you're somewhere where filming yourself might seem a bit awkward, I want you to go where you have privacy or go to a place where you can pretend to be on a video chat with someone. If you simply can't do this exercise right now—perhaps because you're on a train or subway reading this—do this exercise later as homework. But you're more likely to do it if you do so right now.

In a moment, I want you to give a *two-minute elevator pitch about yourself*. It can be about you in your current role or the role you would like to be in or a pitch about your company/employer/organization/school/institution/affiliation.

Don't write notes. Just pick up your phone and video record. (Tip: Turn the phone around so you can't see yourself. Just talk into the camera, not the screen. It'll be less distracting.)

Once you're done, don't watch it yet. Just film for now. Once you're done, put your phone down and come back to this text. Go ahead.

Great job!! I applaud your intrepid nature.

Now you get to do the same thing, but differently. This time I want you to film yourself telling a *two-minute story*. This story has a few requirements. It needs to be (1) about someone you dearly love (child, relative, spouse, partner, bestie, pet); (2) a story to which you have a strong emotional connection (it's hilarious, sad, astonishing, etc.); and (3) a story you remember well enough to easily recall its details.

That's it. Take a moment to think of that story. C'mon. Do it....

Now that you have chosen a story, film yourself again. Don't watch the footage yet—just film. Then come back. I'll wait.

Great job again! I doubly applaud your intrepid nature!

Now you get the opportunity to watch both clips. But let me tell you the things you're not allowed to focus on: what you are wearing, how your hair is styled, or how the room is lit. This is not about focusing on your appearance. Surprisingly, it is also not about focusing on what you actually said. Don't pay attention to all the stuff you said that was dumb or smart or wrong or right.

Instead, I just want you to focus on delivery.

Watch for the speed, pitch, and volume at which you speak; where and for how long you're looking; the enunciation and clarity of your speech; the number of filler words you use; the expressiveness (or not) of your face; the freedom and specificity (or not) of your gestures; your posture; and so forth.

In other words, focus on everything besides what you actually said.

For extra credit, watch them both again with the sound off.

For more extra credit, now play them both again, but turn your screen around so you can't see your image but can only listen to your voice.

Here are my questions for you:

* What did you notice—both good and bad—about your delivery in video 1?
* What did you notice—both good and bad—about your delivery in video 2?
* What were the biggest differences—both good and bad— about your delivery between the two videos?
* On the basis of what you just saw, what is the single biggest overall area for improvement in terms of delivery?

Most likely what you noticed is that video 1 was a lesser version of yourself as compared to video 2: less vocal variety, less facial expressiveness, less gestural freedom, less dynamic enunciation, etc.

Whatever was the single biggest shortcoming that you observed— perhaps even present in both, but possibly more present in video 1 than in video 2—is what I call the low-hanging fruit and the first place I want you to improve in the process of reading and using this book. You have found your first area of focus. Please write that down in the following blank. (Examples: monotone, lack of gestures, slouching.)

My first area of focus is: _____

_____

_____

_____

Congratulations! You have just armed yourself with a powerful new level of awareness. You have closed the perception–reality gap by objectively evaluating yourself with your own eyes and ears. Very likely, in fact, you might already feel empowered to make some positive shifts just from the awareness you gained.

But if you're not feeling empowered—if you didn't like what you saw, or worse you only had all your fears about your "problem areas" confirmed ("I already knew I speak like a runaway freight train!")—never fear! In the very next chapter, we're going to dive into the kinesthetic drills that transform delivery—even stubborn delivery habits that have been accruing for a lifetime.

To get the most out of that chapter—and every one that follows—you need to have some content to use. What do I mean?

Stuff You Can Say

The exercises in this book are effective, and effective quickly. But they are practical drills, not theoretical ones. Therefore, they need practical material with which to … well … practice. You will be prompted in chapter after chapter to "choose some content." So put your imaginary communication scenario hat on and think of various professional settings and the topics about which you communicate in those settings. Here are some basic examples:

- A professional success story
- An update on a multistep project
- An elevator pitch, either about you or your organization
- An overview of an important effort
- An explanation of a mission statement, campaign, or process
- A quarterly review
- An excerpt of a presentation
- A brief bit of thought leadership

I could go on and on. There are, of course, limitless topics with which to practice speaking. So use those as examples, not requirements, and be as creative as you wish.

You may notice that most of those examples tend toward what I would call professional content—"stuff you might talk about at work." That is intentional. For most people, it's important to focus on professional content throughout the exercises of this book, for two reasons: (1) often that is the arena in which people most want to improve; and (2) personal content is often easier to deliver, and if you're trying to grow, it's better to work on the harder stuff. But, please—if you would prefer to apply the lessons and techniques to personal communication content, be my guest!

You'll see those same examples again in Chapter 6 on brevity just as a reminder. But as the chapters move along, I will ask you to "speak some content," knowing that at that point you will have multiple bits of content from which to choose.

Bringing useful, relevant content to practice for every chapter is one of your most important jobs. What are mine? To provide actionable stuff such as the following. Each chapter may include:

+ One or more kinesthetic drills that address that chapter's primary focus
+ Modifications to adapt drills according to individual abilities
+ Instructions for how to weave drills into everyday life
+ Suggestions for how to make drills imperceptible
+ Case studies, stories, and relevant examples
+ QR codes that link to demonstration videos of specific drills
+ Pro tips that offer extra guidance for certain exercises

And to make it fast to flip to a specific skill at any time, I put tabs on the sides of the pages that include the primary focus of that chapter. They may remind you of a dictionary or a reference book. You can use them to quickly navigate or revisit specific lessons and tools. My hope is that soon these pages are as worn and dog-eared as the pages of a well-used travel guidebook.

I will describe each exercise in precise step-by-step instructions that are easy to follow. For those who want even more clarification, demo videos of each chapter's primary exercises can be found at dontsayum.com. You'll be asked to enter your email only once, at which point you'll receive a link giving you access to the guided video curriculum. Once you're logged in, you can dip in and out of the videos and revisit them any time. Your access to these resources doesn't expire. At that URL, you will even get free access to another tool I built for my clients: the GK Training app. It allows you to practice in real time and get instant metrics about your performance. So, if you want to venture to the virtual world to get even more support, it's there.

Once you have learned the tools and drills in each chapter, it is your choice and chance to integrate them into your day. Some drills are for practice; some are for performance. Many can be used for both. Practice drills are intended to be used either solo or with a practice partner outside the actual context of your communication scenario. Think of that like practicing a business pitch on your own or with a friend the day before a big meeting. Performance drills are ones that can be used in a live communication scenario. Making an invisible postural or breath adjustment would be an example of one of those.

You will recognize—often immediately—which drills you should be doing, and doing a lot. When you identify those drills that transform your communication, I suggest practicing them in some manner, ideally even five days a week.

DIFFERENT STROKES FOR DIFFERENT FOLKS

The drills you are about to learn are physical, for all the reasons you now understand from the first five chapters of this book. Because physical bodies are different, various drills may be more or less feasible and more or less relevant to you than others. If some are not feasible for you, no matter! Others will be. Moreover, even the ones that don't seem immediately feasible or relevant may be adjustable or adaptable. Apply the lessons and drills to whatever physical patterns define your life.

As an example, in Chapter 14 on stance and movement, I primarily teach the topics with an assumption of standing on two feet. If you use a wheelchair to move, it's unlikely that you'll relate to some of the descriptions of speakers who endlessly shift their weight or rock back and forth when presenting. But other aspects may still resonate. One example might be the principles of stillness and movement when onstage, in this case manifesting as a chair moving from one portion of the stage to another. Professors use the physical practice of "anchoring" when giving a lecture to symbolize the structure of a topic they're exploring. They may discuss three specific components of a subject standing in three different parts of the lecture hall, respectively. By occupying these distinct locations, the professor helps their students retain the three-part structure of the subject area. Locating ideas in space like that is not limited to those who stand on two legs. The deliberate, methodical movement of a wheelchair across a stage can unlock the same dynamics that a similar move powered by bipedal locomotion can. So I encourage you to challenge yourself to apply the lessons and drills as broadly and creatively as possible.

WHAT ABOUT VIRTUAL?

Because remote communication is such a big part of our lives, where relevant I will examine what changes when we're not in the same space as our audience. But to give you some comfort about the entire topic, let me bat away one concern you might currently have. Besides eye contact—which we will address at length both for live and remote situations in Chapter 12—all the skills you will learn in this book apply to remote communication too. Don't bamboozle yourself; remote communication is not some sort of parallel universe in which all rules are inverted. The task is still the same, though the medium may be different: turn air into audible words and use your voice and body to ensure your audience receives those words.

Your communication is mediated via technology, but that technology is simply the infrastructure. The human communicator in the middle of that infrastructure is still the same. I often tell my clients, "Communication is communication is communication." That is true of remote communication too. In the rare cases that there is a fundamental difference because of the medium, I'll let you know. For now, just take some comfort that, yes, this all applies when on video too, so you don't need to learn all the skills in this book and then go out and learn a whole new set of skills for remote communications. Just read this book and apply what you learn.

In fact, remote situations are ideal scenarios to do just that. Far from being a trap, burden, or minefield, remote communication offers you an incredible gift. It can be a laboratory for you to practice in an invisible way, because it provides what I call a digital "Cloak of Invisibility." No one can see beyond the four borders of your camera's frame. So many of the exercises you're about to learn can be practiced on video calls without your audience knowing. Use that Cloak of Invisibility and transform remote communications from a necessary evil to your practice field.

That's everything you need to know about how to use the chapters that follow.

The first one focuses on conciseness. If you're like most people I've ever coached, it's an essential skill.

Speaking of conciseness: let's begin.

CHAPTER 6

CONCISENESS

How to Talk Less and Say More (and Learn to Pause)

This chapter could also be called, "You ramble too much."

Why is this the place to start?

It's the complaint I hear the most from the managers, HR officers, C-suite leaders, L&D professionals, parents, and deans who hire me to coach: "Michael, [name of the person I'm being asked to coach] could be more concise."

There is an apocryphal story that Ernest Hemingway won a bet regarding who could write the best short story. His buddy wrote a paragraph, Hemingway wrote six words. Although the legend may be baloney, writing a six-word story is an excellent way to explore the power of conciseness. I always asked my students at Columbia to write the six-word story of their lives. I'll share mine with you: "Focusing on others, I found myself." To practice, please write down the six-word story of what brought you to reading this book. Something like "I know I can do better," "Avoiding speaking isn't a winning strategy," or "Facing my fears this time around." Please write your own six-word story here.

_____

_____

If you want to go for extra credit, try for even briefer. One of my favorite bits of brevity I've ever encountered is the tagline of New York City's Mint Theater. It's four words long: "Lost Plays Found Here." They give little-known plays their first American premiere. Want a more well-known four-word story? How about: "First do no harm." Ask someone to tell you the Hippocratic oath, and they'll likely share those four words. But those precise words in that order aren't actually in the Hippocratic oath. This is its own testament to brevity's power: that four-word phrase has so taken root that it has replaced the actual oath.

If you're feeling ambitious, try for four right now!

At its core, achieving conciseness requires you to distill the essence of your idea. We live in an era of attention scarcity. When you have two minutes of an audience's mindshare, you better make it count.

THE OBSTACLE

So, if everyone knows how utterly essential conciseness is, why do people prattle on so?

To explore this, I'm going to ask that you do some talking. In a moment, I want you to speak for approximately two minutes on a *professional topic*. You can use one of the following suggestions, or you can choose something more specific to you. If you're in a private or comfortable place, feel free just to speak out loud. If you are in a very public or shyness-inducing place, then please pick up your phone and pretend you're talking to someone. As a reminder from the previous chapter, here are a few examples of what you could use for content:

- A professional success story
- An update on a multistep project
- An elevator pitch, either about you or your organization

- An overview of an important effort
- An explanation of a mission statement, campaign, or process
- A quarterly review
- An excerpt of a presentation
- A brief bit of thought leadership

In a moment, I just want you to talk out loud for a couple of minutes on any of those topics (or a different one of your choosing). I'm not going to give you any more instruction than that. You might need a pep talk now. There is a very high probability that you're about to risk wasting your time by...*not doing the exercises you are reading this book to learn how to do!*

People often don't do the exercises in books like this. It's like hiring a trainer and then not going to the gym; buying healthy vegetables and not cooking them; getting in bed early enough to be well rested and then doomscrolling through your newsfeed.

This exercise is one of the most transformative in my entire suite. It's not an exaggeration to say it's the foundational drill that launched my exploration of kinesthetic learning in 2009.

If you're tempted to blow off this exercise and just keep reading the book (as flattered as I am that you think I have written a "page-turner")...*don't*. You will get much more out of this book if you do the exercises. I promise you I won't betray your good faith in me by having you do low-impact drills.

The reason it is so essential to do the drills is that if you accept—as I detailed extensively in Chapters 3 and 4—that spoken communication is ultimately a physical art, then not doing these drills is the same as hiring a golf pro and then only listening to what they say without ever picking up a club.

I'm the golf pro; you paid cash money for this book. Let's do this thing!

Ready? Do it now: Talk out loud on one of those topics (success story, project update, elevator pitch, etc.).

*   *   *

Thank you!! Well done!! Now, how can you improve what you just said?

You get to start by defiling a book. Yes! You get to channel your inner three-year-old and tear up a book. Exult in brazen toddlerhood!

Once you flip this page, cut along the dotted lines so that you have six smaller pieces of paper from the single piece of paper that you cut from.

What you're going to do next is called the GK Lego drill. I couldn't put Lego blocks in a book, so we're going to use a page instead. You can also do this drill with sticky notes, but Lego blocks (or Duplo blocks) work best. Once you've tried this version of the drill, I'll show you how it's done with Lego blocks too.

In a moment, I want you to share your same content (whichever of those four prompts you chose) but only one idea at a time. To help you do that, I want you to *rigorously* stick to the instructions I'm about to share. I encourage you to be very disciplined. These techniques are similar to athletic drills. Practicing a basketball shot or a baseball swing only helps if the practice is methodical and focused; so, too, with these drills. Read these instructions first, then try this exercise:

Pick up a piece of paper, and—once you're holding that piece of paper in the air—speak the first thought of your content. As soon as you have completed that thought—in other words, where the period might go at the end of your "first sentence"—place the piece of paper down on the table or desk in silence. Silently pick up the next piece of paper; once that is in the air, you can speak the second thought of your content, but as soon as you have completed that thought (again, where a period might go at the end of the sentence if it were transcribed), place down that second piece of paper, again in silence. Silently pick up the next piece; once aloft, say your third thought. As soon as it's completed, place down the third piece of paper in silence. Silently pick up the fourth piece; begin speaking the fourth thought...and so on and so forth until you've utilized all six pieces. You may not get "all the way through" your content—that's okay! Just keep going and use the six pieces again. Alternatively, you may only need four or five thoughts to complete your content; that is fine too. You might be tempted to cheat in this drill: You may want to place the paper down in the middle of the thought or at random times throughout your content. Resist!

For the drill to be effective, it's essential that you maintain discipline with placing the paper in complete silence at the end of every single thought.

To clarify, what I'm calling one "thought" could also be thought of as one sentence. But we think in thoughts, not sentences. Also, if you notice yourself only using one piece of paper while saying a run-on sentence such as "The project we handled had three main phases we decided to tackle it with a mixture of collaborative work and individual assignments the individuals got to choose some of their work and then others were assigned and from there the project ran smoothly the only thing that was unpredictable was the customer response," you are saying too many thoughts per piece of paper. One piece of paper = one thought.

Okay, ready? Give the drill a try.

Well done! What improvements did you notice? Did you

- Speak for a shorter amount of time?
- Use less filler language?
- Pause more?
- Surprisingly, cover much of what needed to be covered?
- End your sentences with finality instead of trailing off, inflecting up, or adding endless tangents?

In reading the foregoing list, you might agree most of those are positive developments. But there may have been negative ones as well. Perhaps you lost some of the humor or color or your voice was more monotone. Resist the urge to categorize your communication with the reductive and tyrannical titles of good and bad. Notice nuance. Perhaps your structure improved, pausing was better, brevity increased, but vocal variety contracted. Your challenge next time, then, is to keep the improvements and add back in greater vocal variety. This drill is not a panacea. It is a powerful way to learn profound communication principles that people struggle to master, like pausing, structure, and brevity. Most important of all, did you notice how the physical activity of the drill forced your communication to alter in unmistakable ways? This exercise helps many people unlock the Virtuous Cycle of Good Communication we discussed in Chapter 4. In this example it works like this:

Rather than just open your mouth and "start talking," the drill requires that you consider the first thing to say. Without even recognizing it, perhaps, that already launched you in a positive direction. Because you had a clearer initial idea, you were less likely to say *um* as the first word out of your mouth. Because you didn't say *um*, the first word benefited from the breath you didn't waste, so you had more breath to fuel variety in your voice. Because you were focusing on that one idea and not nine, you likely spoke through your first idea in a slower, more deliberate fashion. It likely had less filler language and, therefore, was articulated more accurately and completed in fewer words than the first thought of your initial turn. Then, when you had to place the paper down at the end of that thought, you probably ended the thought with more finality, maybe even avoiding upward inflection, vocal fry, or unnecessary tangents.

The activity of having to pick up the next piece of paper before sharing the next thought allowed you the most precious commodity—time—and so you considered not just what you should say but also what you didn't need to say (and therefore what could be eliminated). As you did each of these physical actions of picking up and placing down the papers in silence, hopefully your content and delivery began to reinforce each other in a virtuous cycle and the pauses gave you an opportunity to think and breathe, and the smarter thoughts that resulted were said with even more breath and commitment.

HOW THIS HELPS AND WHY IT'S EFFECTIVE

Typically, people who struggle with conciseness are given some version of the same bad advice I deconstructed in Chapter 2: thought suppression ("don't ramble"), followed by general advice ("just boil it down"), and mental instructions ("be concise") for a physical activity—talking! Maybe they're told to "just give the high-level overview," "keep it brief," or "we only need a thirty-thousand-foot view." What all that typically translates to in the speaker's mind: talk faster. Their understandable fix-it attempt is an endeavor to speak for a shorter amount of time. "If I only speak for two minutes instead of three, that must mean I was more concise, right?" So, their focus moves to speed instead of efficiency, and they start talking faster. Anyone who can relate to this knows what happens next: The person actually speaks for longer and becomes less concise because when you speak faster you're robbing your brain of the one thing it needs to be a better editor of your words—time!—and so you quickly end up down topic cul-de-sacs that were utterly unnecessary and then add tangents and course corrections just to get back to the main theme. Their goal was fewer words, but all they achieved were faster ones.

Then what advice does the speaker receive? "That was good, but next time you could probably still keep it even more high level." And the speaker leaves the meeting, discouraged with their inability to accomplish the thing they have tried yet again to improve.

If you want to speak more concisely, stop telling yourself to be more concise and instead master this drill!

You'll need props to achieve that mastery. You have officially used the one and only piece of paper in this book supplied for this drill (though I promise I'll let you defile other pages!). The good news is there are other kinesthetic tools that work even more effectively than strips of paper. I recommend two options, though Lego or Duplo blocks are the best. Instead of placing down pieces of paper, stack Lego blocks on top of one another, clicking them together between thoughts, maintaining silence as you connect them. They're the best because the activity of connecting them requires a bit of time that can't be sped up; the interlocking pieces need a moment to click into place.

For the GK Training Lego Drill version of this exercise, gather five or six Lego or Duplo blocks. Pick up a single block in your hand and then deliver the first thought of your content. At the end of that thought, place the block down on the table or desk. Then—in silence—take a second block in your hand before starting your next sentence. Share that next thought. Once you've finished that thought, in silence place the block on the previous one, making sure it clicks in place. Again, the placement of the block can be thought of as the period at the end of the sentence. Repeat for each thought as necessary until you've completed what you want to say. (If you have more than five or six thoughts, just disconnect the stack of blocks and start afresh.)

Resist the temptation to cheat: Don't stack in the middle of the thought or at random times. Maintain your discipline of stacking the block in silence at the end of each thought.

Speaking of cheating, sticky notes are the second option, but they make cheating easier because they don't require time to connect. If you use sticky notes, please take the time to smooth each note deliberately to the table so that the sticky portion adheres fully.

I'm agnostic about which sticky notes and/or toy stacking blocks you use—I just want you to do the drill! If you have Lego blocks and sticky notes at home or work, great! Get stacking! If you want to procure some, do so. Any Lego blocks or sticky notes will do. I care not at all which you use but rather that you use them and therefore get practicing.

Last, let's say you're unable or unmotivated to secure props. You can still practice! Get creative; any tools that you can implement will work: coins, cards, pens, and more. The key here is not which objects you use but rather that you remain disciplined and precise with the activity and therefore benefit from the drill's intervention.

In case you have any questions, you can also see a video demonstration of the exercise at dontsayum.com.

If this drill was useful in improving your structure, brevity, conciseness, and/or comfort with silence, I want you to practice—every day.

PRACTICE OR PERFORMANCE?

The Lego drill is both a practice and performance exercise. Use it in private or in low-consequence situations first. Then transition to imperceptible places. As an example, I once coached a very senior financial professional who tended to rush when nervous. The Lego drill transformed her delivery entirely. But, obviously, stacking Lego blocks in meetings isn't feasible. So she adapted the exercise, and in place of stacking blocks, she pushed her left big toe firmly down in her shoe. She could do this imperceptibly and still benefit from the exercise.

WHAT ABOUT VIRTUAL?

When you're on video calls, you don't even have to worry about shifting the exercise to your toe; just stack the Lego blocks on your desk below your camera's frame. Try this a few times first before you actually use it live on a call and choose a low-stakes call for your first attempt, just so you have a chance to get comfortable with it. It may be too loud and obvious, but once you've done it a few times, you will get more and more fluid with it. Alternatively, you can adjust it to be even more imperceptible if you like and just place your hand down on your desk to represent the block instead of using the real thing.

We're only in Chapter 6 and you already have the keys to the kingdom. Well, actually not the whole kingdom—just the keys to the first brick. But upon that brick, communication empires can be built.

And we're just getting started. The Lego drill likely helped you pause, embrace structure, and be succinct. But it might not have helped you be articulate within a given thought. For that, you'll have to use your fingers...and not just to turn the page. Though, while you're at it, turn the page....

CHAPTER 7

ARTICULATENESS

How to Choose Your Words (and Avoid "Um")

The Lego drill you just learned cures a variety of ills and helps speakers improve the overall structure of what they're saying. We're now going to explore how to achieve structure and precision even within thoughts. The goal of this chapter is what I call linguistic precision.

Linguistic precision simply means being in charge of the words you are choosing. When people first contemplate the level of linguistic precision that I'm about to teach you, they sometimes push back with the old, "But it doesn't feel natural" complaint. And whenever I hear that about linguistic precision, I ever so gently push back in turn and say, "It might not feel natural, but what you're calling natural is actually habitual and maybe even cultural."

In certain circles of Victorian England, speaking with a high degree of linguistic precision was expected. In modern-day British Parliament, if you're accusing a political rival of engaging in a deliberately dispiriting argument, you likely would speak with a high level of linguistic precision. Jumping across the pond, if you were an HR director giving a group of new hires the rundown about company policies around bullying, harassment, and respectful work practices, you'd likely speak with a high level of linguistic precision.

Importantly, this is completely distinct from having a large vocabulary. As an example, one of the coaches who works for my company is a stellar teacher, thinker, and communicator named Shawn Fagan, and in writing a note to one of our clients, he used a twenty-five-cent word I actually had to look up: *sartorial*. As homework, we were recommending our client explore presenting in more structured clothing to investigate what that would do for his posture, and Shawn used *sartorial* to describe the task. It made such an impression on me that I looked up the word.

Perhaps those of you out there who already knew what *sartorial* means are thinking, "I have a better vocabulary than Michael Chad Hoeppner—and he wrote a book on communication!" If that is the case, great—I'm glad you do! May it benefit you and continue to grow over time. If you didn't know what *sartorial* meant and you looked it up, now you know, and you now have a slightly larger vocabulary than two paragraphs ago.

 Either way, I want to draw a distinction between linguistic precision and an extensive vocabulary. One has nothing to do with the other. This is an important distinction because very often people end up being much less linguistically precise because they have a level of embarrassment or even shame about their current vocabulary. They stammer, stall, and trip over their words in a misguided attempt to search for the best possible word or to talk so quickly that people won't notice they can't find the "right" word.

Both strategies are counterproductive.

If you believe you need a better vocabulary, then I invite you to explore that mission concurrently with reading this book. (I'll give you a first challenge: if you don't know what *kinesthetic* means, look it up!) But please don't confuse having an extensive vocabulary with being able to speak with linguistic precision. In fact, one could say the following sentence and still be linguistically precise.

"I want to give you a little advice about your wardrobe, and you might call this...the word is escaping me for a moment—it's a fancy word that means 'related to clothing'...it even...has the connotation of being professorial...it starts with an S, I believe....Well, perhaps it will come to me—let me say it a different way for the time being: I want to give you some wardrobe homework."

Note that in that sentence there are no *ums*, no twice-stated words, no re-re-repeated beginnings of words. It is, in fact, a transparent walk-through of the speaker's journey in attempting to find that word—a linguistically precise walk-through.

The test of linguistic precision is simple: Are you saying the words you want to be saying, or not? Put differently, are you choosing your words, or are you just opening your mouth and seeing what comes out?

What's the test? Filler language. It's one of the prime culprits that leads people to seek my help in the first place. People don't call me up and say, "I would like to be more linguistically precise." They call and say, "I need to stop saying *um/like/kinda/sorta/y'know*."

I hear it so frequently, in fact, that I decided to incorporate the topic into the title of this book.

But as I outlined in the preface, stopping filler is a bad goal. Not only is it thought suppression, but it's also entirely focused on the symptom, not the problem. In fact, if I sold T-shirts, they would say:

FILLER LANGUAGE IS NOT A PROBLEM; IT'S A SYMPTOM.

Now I want you to write that manifesto on this page. Yes, write on this page! Feel the joy and freedom of defacing a book.

_____

If you don't have a pen or pencil with you, trace the letters with your fingernail instead.

FILLER LANGUAGE IS NOT A PROBLEM; IT'S A SYMPTOM

The problem is not the *um*; it's the lack of precision with all the other words around the *um*. When people develop greater precision in choosing and speaking all those words, the *ums* (or whatever filler word they habitually say) go away automatically.

Linguistic precision isn't important because I say it's important. It doesn't come from a communication expert (me) telling people (you) to speak with precision. Linguistic precision comes from a deep human need to carefully and accurately decide which ideas to suggest to another person.

To test this idea, let's bring it back—as I often do—to that tremendously other-focused situation in which you are trying to help your friend in crisis. Imagine they're a bit hysterical in that moment or, alternatively, very down in the dumps. Think about how precisely, accurately, and deliberately you would choose the words needed to reach that person. When you open your mouth and gingerly, tenderly try to tell them that their life is off the rails and you are there to help them get it back, is your speech littered with *ums*? No. In that moment you instantly marshal your concentration to choose the words that particular person needs to hear in that particular moment.

Please know, though, that—despite the title of this book—I am not the "um" police. *Ums* are not a sin. In fact, speakers often use *ums* in subtle ways to let others know they're not done speaking, to lubricate an interaction vocally, to claim the conversational floor, etc.

But people also overuse those examples—and more—as justification for the avalanche of unuseful words and sounds that litter their speech. The most frequent justification I hear is, "I say *um* because I need to think of a word." I'll easily give you a common pattern to watch for in life that swiftly undermines that excuse. The next time you're at a group event in which people introduce themselves one at a time going around the room, note how many people say something like "Hi, my name is, *um*, Michael Chad Hoeppner, and I'm..."

Ostensibly, I am the single most qualified person in the entire world to know my name (after my parents), and yet I put an *um* before it. Did I need that *um* to think of my name?

So I have no interest in eradicating *ums*; I do have an interest in examining them.

MAPPING YOUR FILLER LANGUAGE

Here comes the inevitable question: How much filler language do you use?

To examine that, we first have to agree on the terms. Let's look at two categories—filler sounds and filler words. Filler sounds are *uh, um, eh, em,* and all the other nonword sounds we make as we're meandering our way through our speech. As I will be using it, the term *filler words* refers to fully formed words that meet two conditions:

1. You're not aware how frequently you use them.
2. They're not grammatically necessary.

The reason I'm applying these two conditions is that, technically, any word can be a filler word. *Literally* is a painfully popular one. In fact, I once had a client who tossed the word *viscerally* into his speech approximately every twenty seconds. *Viscerally* would not make the top twenty-five most frequently used filler words list. Yet for this person, it had become a crutch about which he was completely oblivious.

Many of the words that we think of as filler are perfectly useful and necessary words. Consider the differences in the following sentences:

I was like a deer caught in the headlights.
There was a deer, like, caught in the headlights.

A mouse is a kind of mammal.
I kinda have a mouse in my house.

She was all he could think about.
He was all, "I could only think about her."

I'm not trying to be a grammar curmudgeon. Of course we use some of these words in multiple ways for conversational effect, and we might use the word *all* to colloquially mean "said" as part of a freewheeling story-telling style.

But if you find you frequently use words that fulfill those two conditions (you're not aware of them and they're not grammatically necessary), there is a good chance your speech could be significantly more powerful if you increased your intentionality.

A notoriously sneaky category of filler language is what I call conditional language. These are words that are intended to modify and put conditions around statements but that typically are unnecessary and serve only to dilute your communication. These are words like *kinda, sorta, just, little,* and *maybe.* They are pernicious words worth becoming aware of because they may be subtle indicators that you're diminishing your ideas and yourself.

Let's figure it out! Remember in Chapter 5 when you filmed yourself the first time? Reflect back on that. Which filler words did you use and how frequent were your *ums* and *uhs*?

You may have already found that your practice with the Lego drill last chapter has shifted some of those habits. That drill can reduce filler language by helping people consider what they want to say and to do so in a more structured manner. But let's get deeper into filler language by focusing on speaking with precision, even from one word to the next.

LET YOUR FINGERS DO THE WALKING

Like the Lego drill, this next exercise uses embodied cognition to force a dramatic intervention into your habitual relationship to language. I call it Finger Walking, and this is how it works. In a moment I want you to speak on a topic. It can be any subject, but don't choose something you know so intimately that speaking about it is second nature. Remember—take risks here, so choose something a bit challenging.

Once you have determined your topic, I want you to do the following. Speak on that topic, but while doing so, "walk" your fingers across a table or desk. Choose each and every word that leaves your mouth. If you find that you don't know what to say next, pause your fingers, pause your words, and don't continue until you've realized what word you next want to share. I recommend using your index and middle fingers as though those fingers were the legs of a very tiny pedestrian who is making their way across the desk. Please walk your fingers forward only (not back and forth or backward). Once your arm is extended across the desk or table as far as it can go, pause, bring your hand back to where it started, and walk your hand forward again along that same stretch of table, continuing with the rest of your content. You do not need to get obsessively focused on each finger step aligning with your content word by word or syllable by syllable. Just focus on "walking your ideas across the table."

Try the exercise now.

Nice job! If you have the space and privacy to try something more expansive, you can try a variation that brings the same emphasis to choosing every word but gets your full body in on the act.

VARIATION: TAPE WALKING

First, adhere a line of masking tape to the floor, and make the line as long as is manageable for the room. If you don't have any tape, you can also just imagine a very precise line on the floor. Or if you happen to be on a tile or wood floor, there may well be lines within the patterns of the flooring.

Next, you're going to practice speaking on your topic, this time walking with your feet in the identical manner you were previously walking with your fingers, choosing and saying precise and specific words as you do. Take deliberate, methodical steps forward while speaking, using each step to actively choose every single word. The image to keep in mind is a gymnast walking along a balance beam, placing the feet as carefully as possible. Another useful image is of a ballerina tiptoeing through a field of lilies, trying not to disturb a single petal of any flower. As with the previous drill, don't get preoccupied evaluating whether each step corresponds to a word or a syllable but rather think very concretely about walking your ideas across the room. Like the finger version of the drill, only move in a forward direction. When you reach the end of the tape, stop, turn around, and begin walking back on the line again. I encourage you to be disciplined with the drill. To ensure you get its full value, challenge yourself to step and speak on the first word in absolute unison. That first step will help you start off "on the right foot." Try it now if you want.

What did you discover? How drastically did your filler change using the Finger Walking or Tape Walking exercise? A bit? A lot? Totally transformed? Or you may have seen, in fact, that filler language was already slightly less present than it was in Chapter 5 when you did your first baseline, simply as a function of building new communication muscles through kinesthetic learning.

But if you're not able to succeed at increasing your linguistic precision yet, don't worry. You just learned the drill. Like the Lego drill last chapter, I invite you to practice the Finger Walking drill (or Tape Walking) a lot: daily, in low-consequence situations, and in imperceptible settings. Speaking of which...

WHAT ABOUT VIRTUAL?

Video calls—where your hand can move outside the camera's frame—are an ideal setting to practice. And speaking of practice...

PRACTICE OR PERFORMANCE?

This drill is both a practice and a performance drill. Begin by using it for practice only because the initial stages can sometimes create a slightly stiffer pattern of delivery as the laser focus on word choice restricts the vocal variety and flow you might typically exhibit. But as you master the exercise, you will be able to use it as a performance one as well, provided you can make the Finger Walking imperceptible. The more you practice, the better your form.

But be nice to yourself as you do, because the final thought I'll add in this chapter is this: Cut yourself some slack. There is a very good chance that the filler language you habitually use is more bothersome to you than to your audience. Let me offer some math to comfort you on this point. On average, speakers of English say approximately three words per second. The average number of syllables per word is a little less than two. (These averages are quite loose, but for the purposes of this equation they're close enough.) That means that within an average second of speaking, your audience is hearing roughly six syllables. Let's imagine you say *um* every five seconds. That frequency probably strikes you as disastrous. But taken as a ratio of the total number of syllables during that span, it's only one syllable for every thirty, or slightly more than 3 percent. I'm guessing you'd be relatively forgiving of yourself for a habit that affected only 3 percent of a given thing. I invite you to embrace that same forgiveness here. Should you strive to reduce your overall habits of filler language? Yes. Should you beat yourself up in that process? No.

Just keep on trucking on your communication-improvement highway and include linguistic precision as one of the attractions along the way. What are the other attractions? Turn the page to find out.

CHAPTER 8

ENUNCIATION

How to Speak Clearly (and Avoid Mumbling)

D o you remember Jim, who used the slice of cork to improve his communication? We're going to learn that exercise now, but with a variation because I can't print an actual wine cork in this book.

This exercise follows the chapter on linguistic precision because, now that you've built greater skill in choosing the precise words you want to share, it's good to learn how to enunciate those words clearly and powerfully.

As I shared in the story about Jim, this drill uses the principle of resistance training to improve communication. The cork serves as an impediment to force your mouth to work harder to get your words past the obstacle. Over time—just like an athlete using resistance training—your enunciation muscles actually get stronger. But there are also instant benefits. One of them is obvious for those fast talkers among you: it makes your speech slower.

The physics behind the effectiveness of this drill are breathtakingly simple: with a cork in your mouth, it takes longer for your lips to come together to make a *p* or *b*, for example, and it takes longer for your tongue to reach up to the dental ridge for a *t* or *d*.

Ever tried to walk somewhere quickly while trudging through calf-deep snow? It's the same idea. If done correctly, this change in your speech could simply be labeled enunciation, defined by Merriam-Webster's as "to say or pronounce clearly." But enunciation is not important because the High Tea etiquette teacher will be upset if you don't enunciate. It is important because enunciation provides you the physical ability to make your ideas, thoughts, desires, and needs known. Enunciation gives you the capability to percussively communicate all manner of complex requests and then get those requests fulfilled!

I recognize you might be thinking, "Sure. But don't people generally understand me fine even if I do say some words quickly or mumble a bit?"

The answer to that question is *perhaps*. Perhaps they do. If you consistently say these two words in such a way that your listener doesn't misconstrue your meaning, then perhaps.

CAN   CAN'T

If a listener hearing you say the following nine *M* words had absolute clarity on the differences of each, then your *perhaps* moves to *definitely*:

MA   MOCK   MOTH

MOP   MOSS   MAW

MOD   MOSH   MAUVE

Enunciation matters. It obviously determines whether you can be understood or not, but it goes deeper.

Remember the term *onomatopoeia* from high school English class? Onomatopoeia means words that sound like the things they represent. Again, according to Merriam-Webster's, the full definition is "the formation of a word from a sound associated with what is named." *Cuckoo, babble, sizzle, slap, splash, warble, gurgle, mumble,* and *flop* are some recognizable examples. But going a bit deeper, consider words like *bell* and *snake*. Note how the activity of saying the word *bell* is not unlike the action of striking a bell. The *b* is a voiced consonant that is struck a single time and can't be sustained (like the striking of a bell); the short *e* contains no diphthong, so it remains as a single pure sound (like the single pure note of a bell); the *l* can be sustained and then slowly recede into silence, like the fading sound of the bell strike resolving. There is a reason a "bell" is not called a "thud."

How about *snake*? The consonant and vowel sounds help the listener understand what they're dealing with: the sustained *s* mimics the hiss of the snake itself, the diphthong curves between two vowel sounds just as the snake curves, and the percussive *k* gives the listener a fast, final encounter with the end of the word, in hopes they won't have a similarly fast, final encounter with that particular animal!

Take a moment—if you haven't—and say these two words slowly, noting how the sounds evoke the meaning of the words. Slow the words down.

Say Be*LLLLLLLLLL*.

Now say sssssssssssssssna**KE**

Feel how physical enunciation truly is? The *b* in *bell* is the tolling of a large bell atop a steeple. The hard *k* at the end of *snake* is the strike of a serpent on your bootless leg. (These are examples in English. You can find words like these in other languages, of course, too.)

People recognize that gestures and posture are physical—but enunciation is just as physical. And because it's physical, like any other activity, from tying shoelaces to knitting a scarf, it can be practiced and improved, regardless of how squirrelly your mind might be in that moment. You can become a more powerful speaker just by doing your exercises.

The last benefit of enunciation I will point out is that powerful enunciation can even help you make fewer mistakes.

I'll share more about this in future chapters, but often when humans are trying to avoid speech mistakes, they make the exact wrong adjustment: They contract and close their mouths in an effort to keep the wrong word or sound from escaping. What this does is increase the likelihood they'll say an inaccurate sound. It's much easier to let a *d* become a *j* if your tongue has almost no room to move. Counterintuitively, if you take the risk to open your mouth more and make all your sounds more fully, you are actually lowering your articulators' level of difficulty.

You can try the following fun exercise to experience the effect. With the tip of your finger, please touch each of the dots in series 1 and then do the same in series 2. Please touch the dots as precisely as possible, and only touch each dot once.

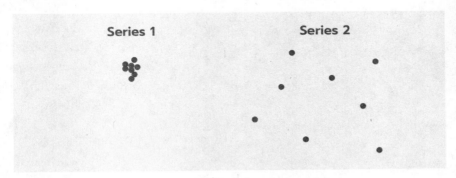

The difficulty your finger just experienced in trying to precisely touch the dots in series 1 is the same difficulty you're giving your tongue when you try to speak with very little space in your mouth. Using the cork impediment forces you to practice speaking with more room in your mouth.

If you have a wine cork handy, excellent! Please lay it on a flat cutting surface and carefully slice a piece off the end, approximately this wide [—]. (Disclaimer: please be careful when cutting!)

If you don't have a cork, I've provided a substitute. On the next page you'll see a series of dotted lines. Just like folding a piece of origami or paper airplane, this page is intended to be torn out and folded up into a small rectangle about this size:

If you want to use an actual wine cork, please do. There is one legal matter I must emphasize about that tool though: Do not inhale and choke on the cork! Keep hold of it on the side with your fingers as you speak so you anchor it. It is hard to improve your communication if you have a slice of wine cork lodged in your throat. If you have even the slightest concern about using the cork, you can substitute any number of other objects for the same purpose:

- The tip of your little finger
- The end of a pen or pencil
- A piece of gum still in the wrapper
- A mint
- A rolled-up piece of gauze or fabric

(In fact, if you want a chuckle, scan this QR code and watch my then five-year-old son use a magnetic tile as an impediment.)

But whatever tool you're using, your job is the same: Enunciate as much as is necessary to be understood flawlessly, even while fighting past the impediment in between your teeth. Here are the step-by-step instructions to the drill, the principle of which goes back thousands of years (and probably longer than that).

Place the cork (or other impediment) between your top and bottom teeth, slightly off to the side. Keep your lips open. Speak while keeping the cork between your teeth. Work as hard as is necessary to make sure each and every word is completely intelligible. If you're with a partner, speak to your partner and see if they can understand everything. If you're by yourself, record yourself using the voice recorder on your phone, then listen back and note whether you can understand everything. You can also

use any voice-to-text transcription tool (including the GK Training app you have access to at dontsayum.com) and see whether it can accurately document your words. You might even find you prefer the way you sound with the cork in terms of pace, resonance, and diction! Now remove the cork and see if you can retain that powerful, deliberate enunciation without the cork. Move back and forth between using and not using the cork so that you can soon blend the two together and ensure deliberate, clear speech even without the impediment.

Try it now, recording yourself as you do.

PRO TIP

An important pitfall to avoid in this drill is the trap of not sufficiently altering your speech to compensate for the cork. People sometimes mumble through what they're saying without actually using their lips in a more decisive way. To help, move your lips in as exaggerated a manner as necessary to make sure that every single letter in every single word is entirely clear. In fact, it's not "too much" if your lips even move out around the cork and meet on the outside of the cork for consonants like *p*, *b*, and *m*. As with the other slightly outside-the-box drills, you may gently resist this because of the slight suspicion of looking silly. But the payoff, when the drill is done correctly, is incredible. It's worth persevering through the mild discomfort to realize the benefit.

PRACTICE OR PERFORMANCE?

This drill is obviously for practice only, not performance. Talking with a cork in between your teeth at an important meeting might raise more than a few eyebrows. But if you're trying to improve your enunciation skills, practice this drill at least five minutes two times a day every day. Don't let being busy be an obstacle! I've had clients squeeze this practice into their day in the most innovative ways. My favorite zero-brain-power way is this: After you brush your teeth in the morning and at night, use the head of your toothbrush as an impediment. In the morning talk about what your day has in store, and at night talk about what your day delivered. Heck, you might even grow to love that ritual on its own, separate from the enunciation benefits. That would be an unexpected positive outcome, wouldn't it?

WHAT ABOUT VIRTUAL?

Video calls can provide an opportunity to be extra mindful of your enunciation. Try this exercise. The next time you're on a video call, look at your own video box while speaking. You can literally watch your enunciation and evaluate it in real time. Can you see frequent black space between your top and bottom teeth as your mouth and lips move expressively? There's a good chance your enunciation is working well. Not seeing any space between your top and bottom teeth? Likely your audience is not receiving the benefit of your ideas.

Dynamic enunciation—whether verified by watching yourself on video or cultivated by fighting past a cork—affects your rate of speech for a simple reason: It takes time to speak clearly. Rate of speech can also be referred to as pace—and it's one of the Five Ps of Vocal Variety. What is vocal variety, and what are the other four Ps? You'll find out in the next chapter.

CHAPTER 8 ENUNCIATION

CHAPTER 9

VOCAL VARIETY

How to Speak Expressively (and Avoid Monotone)

Welcome to the longest chapter in *Don't Say Um*. Be not dismayed! Long does not equal boring in this case; long equals important.

This chapter is the remedy for all the ridiculous pablum you have probably encountered on this topic before. The subject is often brushed over with such an inadequate, dismissive, and anti-productive brush that it is distilled into one word—*tone*—and speakers are given utterly useless advice like "drop into your authenticity" or "be more passionate" or "give me some positivity."

In this chapter, we are not going to do any of this: ~~drop into your authenticity~~ or ~~be more passionate~~ or ~~give me some positivity.~~

We are going to take a practical, rigorous, and comprehensive approach to unlocking one essential aspect of speaking, because it warrants it.

To start, I want to ask you a question, and I want you to be honest with me (and yourself). *Have you been doing the exercises in this book?* Did you do the filming exercise I suggested in Chapter 5, the multiple paper-tearing or folding activities, the talking out loud when prompted, and more?

First, if you have been doing the activities, *rock on*! Good job!

If not, reflect for a moment: Why haven't you done the activities yet?

I'm not asking to make you feel guilty. I have no interest in creating guilt—there is enough of that in the world! Let's skip the guilt and just get straight to examining one of the obstacles that prevents people from embracing the activities and exercises. (And thereby hopefully remove that obstacle.)

There are many causes for inaction or procrastination, but I want to focus on a particular one in this chapter. To do that, please fill in the following sentence. You can write on the page or just say it out loud:

When I hear my own voice played back to me it's _____

_____

_____

_____

Typically, when I do this exercise with clients, the things I hear are relentlessly self-critical: "like nails on a chalkboard," "annoying," "abrasive," "too nasal," "alien," "like a foghorn." You may have written something similarly harsh.

Many, many, many of us report not liking the sound of our own voice. This is a difficult state of affairs. One's voice is a very personal thing. It has to do with

- Where you grew up (Do you have an accent? Depends on where you are in the world...and who's evaluating.)
- How you use your body (Remember Chapter 2? Spoken communication is physical, and it changes depending on how you use your diaphragm, lungs, torso, throat, mouth, lips, and more.)
- How much you open your mouth (Afraid of letting something slip that you shouldn't?)
- How your family and friends speak (Have family issues? Welcome to the club.)
- Your culture (Always over-the-top? Or, alternatively, have a hard time speaking up?)
- How you breathe (Or don't.)

+ What you have said—and have been punished or praised for (Both can create challenges.)
+ What you haven't said (Regret much?)

Given all that, it's no wonder it can feel vulnerable to hear and examine one's voice.

But before you retreat into a fixed mindset that has confined and condemned your voice, let me gently question your assumptions about what a voice is. It may not be the common noun you think. People speak about their voice as though it were an object—and a static object at that. "I have a [squeaky, shrill, monotone, boring, scratchy] voice," the lament goes. In truth, you don't have a [squeaky, shrill, monotone, boring, scratchy] voice; you have an endlessly flexible voice. And if you don't like your voice, there's a very high likelihood it's not actually your voice!

What the heck do I mean by that? Modern society conspires to compromise our ability to create sound freely and healthfully. If you recall the thought experiment from Chapter 3, which of these two people would still have a voice left after screaming from ten at night to six in the morning?

(Hint: it's not the person with the bullhorn.)

 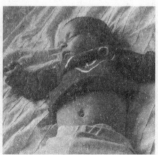

We adjust and corrupt our voices for a variety of reasons as we move through life. So, if you don't like your voice, never fear! It's not your real voice anyway.

I don't say that to sound glib but rather to create a little space in your consciousness to be nicer to yourself as you examine expanding the way in which you speak.

You can get a hint of this even by considering the title of one of the most legendary vocal training books of the last century, *Freeing the Natural Voice*, by Kristin Linkletter. Note that the title isn't "Taming the Natural Voice" or "Strengthening the Natural Voice."

So instead of fixating on how bad you think you sound on *video* or in a *voice mail* or in your voicemail *greeting*, instead think about how different your voice sometimes sounds

- After you've had a good cry
- Upon waking from a long, relaxing nap
- After a couple of glasses of wine
- On a late-night phone call with a long-distance romantic partner

The sound of your voice can change—and change dramatically. In fact, it does change, and—like most every other example in this book—it changes organically and instinctually when you are solely focused on reaching the other person.

How specifically does it change? It's what I call *vocal variety*. That term might be new to you, but the topic isn't, because people talk about it all the time, just in different terms. If you have heard people speak about "tone of voice," "monotone," "shrill," or any number of other descriptions or critiques of voices, they're talking about vocal variety.

In working with speakers for fifteen years, I have developed an alliterative system of Five Ps to help clients understand, remember, and eventually unlock greater vocal variety. The Five Ps are as follows:

- Pace (fast and slow)
- Pitch (high and low)
- Pause (musical rest)
- Power (loud and soft)
- Placement (where the sound amplifies in the body)

Looking at those five, you probably intuitively recognize the categories and glimpse the interconnectedness. The only one you may have a bit of confusion about is *placement*. If you know a friend who has a very nasal voice, technically what's happening is the sound of their voice is amplifying primarily in the nasal cavities of their head and face rather than throughout the rest of their body. That's called placement—the sound is "placed" in the nasal "mask" area of the face.

For musicians, these five dynamics will be instantly recognizable—they're what they know well as dynamics in musical composition. Power (volume) in musical scoring is indicated, of course, by the term *pianoforte* (loud) and *pianissimo* (soft). The other Ps all map neatly as well. Pitch is as it sounds—the musical note high or low on the scale. Pace is tempo and rhythm. Pause is the frequency, pattern, and length of the various rests. And when a performer puts a mute in their trumpet or closes the lid on the harp of their piano, they have altered placement, when the manipulation of the instrument's architecture affects where the sound amplifies.

Just learning about this system can be a revelation for people who struggle with vocal variety—musicians and nonmusicians alike. Consider those who have been told they have a monotone voice (or even more reductively, "you're monotone"—as though monotone were a nationality or race). These people have often endured decades of being told "you sound bored," "just speak with more passion," and "you don't seem enthusiastic," or (worst of all) of being deprived of speaking opportunities because—as one of my clients was told—"you put the audience to sleep." When they learn this system of Five Ps, people who are tremendous achievers but who have never been able to communicate about those achievements with energy and enthusiasm realize that there are specific measurements to evaluate against and then improve.

But as powerful as that revelation is, it's nothing compared to the aha moment they experience when they actually learn how to unleash the Ps. Working with other academics around the country—social scientists and management professors at Ivy League institutions and large research universities—we used this framework of Five Ps to examine politicians' speeches. This analysis enabled us to offer some key findings in distilled form to political figures, the names of whom you would recognize. I give you that slightly obnoxious, anonymized, name-dropping context for an important reason: The most seasoned, powerful political communicators in the world need this kind of help too. If you know that you could use more vocal variety and/or convey more enthusiasm, drama, or passion, it's not that something is wrong with you. Many people have room for improvement, just like those brand-name politicians.

We used my system of Five Ps to examine a specific politician's patterns and identified that this person was particularly challenged in varying power and pitch. I even documented the pattern visually, because the WAV files of the voice look entirely different when the speaker is using vocal variety effectively versus when not.

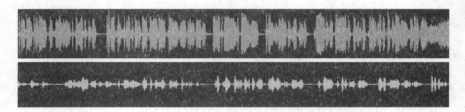

Notice how in the first illustration each time the speaker says a word it shows up as a "blob" of sound, and all the blobs appear at repetitive intervals and at the same amplitude. Compare it to the second illustration, in which the amount of space in between blobs is varied, some blobs are thin and tall, some are short and long, some are barely a ripple, some look like a sunfish.

What you're looking at is the visual representation of the variety in the speaker's voice. The first illustration is taken from a particularly ineffective speech when the candidate blared loudly and repetitively most of the time. The second is from an event in which the candidate spoke with much more variety, nuance, and subtlety. Shocker—the audience responded more positively at the second event.

Put as simply as possible, what our examination of vocal variety using my Five Ps dynamic framework revealed is this: Speakers who use vocal variety come across better than those who don't. They are assigned a variety of positive attributes by their audience: trustworthy, credible,

CHAPTER 9
VOCAL VARIETY

thoughtful, persuasive, and more.[1-7] Hopefully, that snapshot of the research is intriguing for you, but there is a good chance you already possess this insight. The cliché of the droning, monotonous politician is so engrained in our traditions of comedy and parody that it's almost become a stock character. Look no further than the long-running TV show *The Simpsons* and its monotone Mayor Quimby of Springfield character. The inauthenticity is the point.

VOCAL VARIETY—ESSENTIAL AND INNATE

I showed you some science to intrigue your brain, I've made them all Ps to activate your appetite for alliteration, and I shared a story to engage your empathy. So, hopefully, you'll remember these Five Ps.

But the great news is this: You don't have to remember them. In fact, you never have to even think about them again, because you already know

1   M. K. Surawski and E. P. Ossoff, "The Effects of Physical and Vocal Attractiveness on Impression Formation of Politicians," *Current Psychology* 25, no. 1 (2006): 15–27.

2   M. G. Boltz, "Temporal Dimensions of Conversational Interaction: The Role of Response Latencies and Pauses in Social Impression Formation," *Journal of Language and Social Psychology* 24, no. 2 (2005): 103–138.

3   J. Schroeder and N. Epley, "The Sound of Intellect," *Psychological Science* 26 (2015): 877–891; and J. Schroeder and N. Epley, "Mistaking Minds and Machines: How Speech Affects Dehumanization and Anthropomorphism," *Journal of Experimental Psychology* 145, no. 11 (2016): 1427–1437.

4   J. T. Cheng, J. L. Tracy, S. Ho, and J. Henrich, "Listen, Follow Me: Dynamic Vocal Signals of Dominance Predict Emergent Social Rank in Humans," *Journal of Experimental Psychology: General* 145, no. 5 (2016): 536.

5   S. W. Gregory and T. J. Gallagher, "Spectral Analysis of Candidates' Nonverbal Vocal Communication: Predicting U.S. Presidential Election Outcomes," *Sociology and Psychology Quarterly* 65 (2002): 298–308.

6   C. Gelinas-Chebat and J. C. Chebat, "Effects of Two Voice Characteristics on the Attitudes Towards Advertising Messages," *Journal of Social Psychology* 132 (1992): 447–459; and C. Gelinas-Chebat, J. C. Chebat, and A. Vaninsky, "Voice and Advertising: Effects of Intonation and Intensity of Voice on Source Credibility, Attitudes Toward the Advertised Service and the Intent to Buy," *Perceptual and Motor Skills* 104 (1996): 419–437.

7   M. Zuckerman and K. Miyake, "The Attractive Voice: What Makes It So?" *Journal of Nonverbal Behavior* 17, no. 2 (1993): 119–135; and M. Zuckerman, H. Hodgins, and K. Miyake, "The Vocal Attractiveness Stereotype: Replication and Elaboration," *Journal of Nonverbal Behavior* 14, no. 2 (1990): 97–112.

them, and you know them in your bones. To prove this to you, I want you to imagine saying these eight words to a three-year-old while trying to do a time-tested switcheroo trick:

DO YOU WANT THIS THING OR *THIS THING*?

Let's imagine the three-year-old has picked up some stranger's cell phone, and you're trying to get it back. All you have to trade is a ball. How might you use vocal variety to make the ball sound like much more fun than the cell phone? Hear yourself saying those words. Do you change pace? Probably, likely slowing down to feature the ball. Do you change pitch? You probably emphasize the ball over the phone by raising or lowering your pitch. Do you use power? I bet you do. For the object you're trying to engender interest in, you probably speak a bit louder. Do you use pause? Yep. You probably pause to create some suspense in unveiling the ball. And I bet you would even shift placement. Indicating the phone, you might resonate more nasally or alternatively in the back of the throat to communicate disregard. Relating to the ball, you might resonate sound throughout your entire body to communicate wonder. You know all these Five Ps unthinkingly. We all do.

These Ps are so ingrained in us, in fact, that all of them are quite interconnected. More, it's very challenging to change only one of them in isolation from the others. If you don't believe me, just try it!

But the benefit of a single aspect of vocal variety being difficult to change in isolation is that it gives you an easy way to begin the journey of embracing more. If you know that you tend to speak in a monotonous voice—which technically is a lack of variety in pitch—how great is it that if you just practice using louder and softer power, faster and slower pace, and longer and shorter pausing, pitch will automatically begin to modulate too, simply because they're all deeply interconnected?

Lack of vocal variety can also be seen not only within a sentence but also as a pattern that affects *each* sentence. Perhaps you repetitively inflect up at the end of each sentence, or alternatively, you trail off (habits we will examine in greater depth next chapter). The result of these patterns is that each thought sounds equivalent to all the others. Your speech therefore sounds less other-focused and more self-focused, slightly autopilot, and definitely repetitive.

Consider written language for a moment. In English, there are eight ways to indicate an end or pause. They are the following:

1. Period (.)
2. Comma (,)
3. Colon (:)
4. Semicolon (;)
5. Ellipsis (...)
6. Exclamation point (!)
7. Question mark (?)
8. Dash (—)

If you repetitively end a sentence in the same way, it is the equivalent of doing the following to your speaking:

To be, or not to be? That is the question? Whether 'tis nobler in the mind to suffer the slings and arrows of outrageous fortune? Or to take arms against a sea of troubles, and by opposing end them? To die? To sleep? No more?[1]

Alternatively, if you trail off relentlessly, that might be the equivalent of doing this:

To be, or not to be.... That is the question.... Whether 'tis nobler in the mind to suffer the slings and arrows of outrageous fortune.... Or to take arms against a sea of troubles, and by opposing end them.... To die.... To sleep.... No more....[2]

When humans are at their other-focused best, they tend to use a wide variety of intonations and rhythms throughout thoughts to make sounds

---

1   William Shakespeare, *Hamlet*, Act III, Sc. 1.
2   William Shakespeare, *Hamlet*, Act III, Sc. 1.

distinct from one another. Once again, imagine talking to your friend in crisis. You can imagine the punctuation of that dialogue looking like the following (I've bolded each of those eight punctuation marks so you can note their usage):

> It's going to be okay**!** You think I'm going to let you talk to your-self this way**?** The first thing we're going to do is start a list**;** we're going to write down the very best outcome that can happen**—** and the very worst**.** You can go into as much detail as you want**:** every little terrifying thing you're worried about**,** or just the giant worst-case scenarios**....**

Notice how each of those punctuation marks suggests a different use of vocal variety to let the listener know your tone and intention and maybe even preview where you're going next.

THE PURPOSES OF VOCAL VARIETY

Vocal variety is not accidental. It is not just "nice to have." It is essential and has multiple purposes. Vocal variety: (1) indicates emotion; (2) conveys meaning; (3) orients the listener; and (4) surprises the audience.

Indicate Emotion

Indicating emotion is the purpose of vocal variety with which you're already very familiar. We've all learned this lesson about emotion the hard way. If you need an instant, vivid demonstration, just look at the following figure.

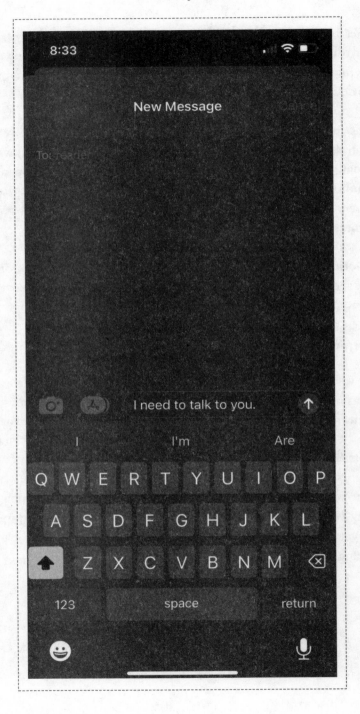

With what vocal variety did you just hear my voice in your head? Was I mad at you? Ashamed by you? Abhorred by your behavior? Excited to share more information with you about vocal variety? Interested in making lunch plans next week? In dire need of some tax documents from you?

If you've ever misread the intention of a text message, you have been the victim of inaccurate vocal variety as you played that person's voice in your head. Perhaps you thought they were furious with you, and it turns out they were just trying to get confirmation about something.

You're already so familiar with this purpose that you probably even have some insight into how the Ps change depending on the emotional tone of the speaker (that is, power is often louder when angry or pace is faster when excited).

You may not be as familiar with the other purposes though.

Convey Meaning

Vocal variety also communicates meaning. Consider this old emphasis game, using the phrase "I did not steal your red pen."

If you say, "I did not steal your *red* pen," the implication, of course, is that you stole the other-colored pen (maybe blue). But if you say, "I did not steal your red *pen*," the implication might be that you stole the red pencil. Or if you say, "I did not *steal* your red pen," the implication is that you just borrowed it.

For a slightly absurd example, consider one of the cliché archetypes of modern speech: the often-ridiculed Valley Girl pattern of speech, in which everything is personification and single-syllable words. Imagine trying to make sense of the following sentence if the speaker wasn't using vocal variety to communicate both tone and meaning.

> "She was like 'no way!' and I was all like 'way.' And then they were all 'what?' and she was like 'I know…'"

Orient the Listener

To understand how vocal variety orients a listener, let's consider a series of ordered sounds that doesn't even feature words: speaking a telephone number.

When I tell someone my phone number, I say it in a musical pattern, something like this:

What's going on here?

It would be understandable to think that humans speak a phone number in a monotone—slowly, clearly, and evenly, with each digit being identical in terms of pace, pitch, pause, power, and placement. You're just saying numbers, right? The different identity of each of the digits should be sufficient for comprehension. That might look like this.

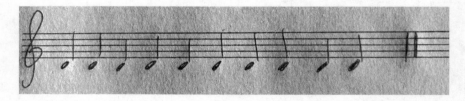

But this is not how we generally speak phone numbers—or Social Security numbers or our birthdays in eight-digit form or postal codes or all manner of number series. Humans tend to inflect the numbers up and down on a musical scale, anchoring our ears to the similar and different notes. By "playing the same note," you are indicating to your audience the identical value of the digit. Think of the musical passage of my phone number as something akin to this (with each of the repeated words representing the same number): **identical**, *same*, **identical**—DIFFERENT, *same*, **novel**—*same*, *fresh*, <u>distinct</u>, unique. In that passage, you might imagine a number like this: 646-247-4803 (sincere apologies if I have just shockingly guessed your phone number. Readers—please don't dial that number! I just made it up, but some poor soul somewhere is probably the possessor of that phone number. Though the sheer curiosity may be excruciating to resist, don't phone them! None of us need more random, unnecessary phone calls!)

Let's examine that same musical representation of that phone number again.

Notice a few things. Notice how the identical numbers tend to map to the same note: in this case the 6s and 4s. Pitching the same number identically helps your listener instantly recognize that those numbers repeat, thereby helping the listener digest and retain the number. Notice how digits that are unique get pitched apart from others; an 8 doesn't get the same pitch as a 2. Notice how there are two musical rests—pauses, in other words. Note that they coincide precisely with the typical gaps in the written representation of a phone number, typically indicated either with hyphens or parentheses, like (646) 247-4803. We pause there to help people digest the series in brief groupings—two groupings of three numbers and one of four. Those pauses aid our retention. It also prompts our recognition that we are being offered something quite familiar—a phone number—and we can categorize it in the same way as every other ten-digit phone number we have ever received. My transcription is a faithful if not flawless representation of how I tend to say that number series. I could be even more rigorous and add additional nuance. On the third and sixth note I tend to do the slightest inflection up in pitch to preview that more notes are to come. I tend to adjust power as well to increase the emphasis on the numbers that don't repeat. I haven't indicated those micro-variations here, because I'm not scoring a symphony, just illustrating a point.

If we use vocal variety with this much subtlety and sophistication in speaking something as pedestrian as a phone number, imagine how sophisticated our use of it must be when saying actual words.

Surprise the Audience

In addition to orienting and conveying meaning and emotion, humans also use vocal variety to continually surprise one another. Whether you're aware of it or not, your brain is wired to look for surprises. It burns an outsized amount of your total calories given its fairly minor weight (approximately three pounds); therefore, your body is always looking for moments to power it down and conserve calories. When is it safe to power down? When all observable surroundings are predictable and orderly. The moment your brain recognizes a pattern, it can dedicate less and less attention to it until eventually you may not even register it at all. Think of an electric fan whirring in the background—eventually, the sound becomes white noise, and our brains don't even note it.

This adaptation is important from an evolutionary standpoint; it conserves energy for the sprint away from the inevitable, lurking saber-toothed tiger. A surprise can signal danger—in the case of the prehistoric predator—or delight. It is something unexpected and our brains have to focus on it very quickly to determine its implications. To examine this, try this thought experiment:

- You open the door of your home. SURPRISE! It's a birthday party for you! All your nearest and dearest are there.
- You open the door of your home. SURPRISE! You left the burner on and there is a fire on your stovetop!

In both those opposing situations of delight and danger, reflect on how much your brain attends to the situation.

Or compare an expected event to a surprising one. To make this experiential, in a moment I want you to consider the expected event of the next two pages. Notice which of the two pages grabs your attention more. Ready? Turn the page.

Lorem ipsum lorem ipsum lorem ipsum lorem ipsum lorem ipsum lorem
ipsum lorem ipsum lorem ipsum lorem ipsum lorem ipsum lorem ipsum
lorem ipsum lorem ipsum lorem ipsum lorem ipsum lorem ipsum lorem
ipsum lorem ipsum lorem ipsum lorem ipsum lorem ipsum lorem ipsum
lorem ipsum lorem ipsum.

Lorem ipsum lorem ipsum lorem ipsum lorem ipsum lorem ipsum
lorem ipsum lorem ipsum lorem ipsum lorem ipsum lorem ipsum lorem
ipsum lorem ipsum Lorem ipsum lorem ipsum lorem ipsum lorem ipsum
lorem ipsum lorem ipsum lorem ipsum lorem ipsum lorem ipsum lorem
ipsum lorem ipsum lorem ipsum lorem ipsum lorem ipsum lorem ipsum
lorem ipsum lorem ipsum lorem ipsum lorem ipsum lorem ipsum lorem
ipsum lorem ipsum lorem ipsum lorem ipsum lorem ipsum lorem ipsum
lorem ipsum lorem ipsum lorem ipsum lorem ipsum lorem ipsum lorem
ipsum lorem ipsum lorem ipsum lorem ipsum.

Lorem ipsum lorem ipsum lorem ipsum lorem ipsum lorem ipsum
lorem ipsum lorem ipsum lorem ipsum lorem ipsum.

Lorem ipsum lorem ipsum lorem ipsum lorem ipsum lorem ipsum
lorem ipsum lorem ipsum lorem ipsum lorem ipsum lorem ipsum Lorem
ipsum lorem ipsum lorem ipsum lorem ipsum lorem ipsum lorem ipsum
lorem ipsum lorem ipsum lorem ipsum lorem ipsum lorem ipsum lorem
ipsum lorem ipsum lorem ipsum.

Lorem ipsum lorem ipsum lorem ipsum lorem ipsum lorem ipsum
lorem ipsum lorem ipsum lorem ipsum lorem ipsum lorem ipsum lorem
ipsum lorem ipsum lorem ipsum lorem ipsum lorem ipsum lorem ipsum
lorem ipsum lorem ipsum lorem ipsum lorem ipsum lorem ipsum lorem
ipsum lorem ipsum lorem ipsum lorem ipsum lorem ipsum lorem ipsum
lorem ipsum lorem ipsum lorem ipsum

Lorem ipsum lorem ipsum lorem ipsum lorem ipsum lorem ipsum
lorem ipsum lorem ipsum lorem ipsum lorem ipsum lorem ipsum lorem
ipsum lorem ipsum lorem ipsum lorem ipsum lorem ipsum lorem ipsum
lorem ipsum lorem ipsum lorem ipsum lorem ipsum lorem ipsum lorem
ipsum lorem ipsum lorem ipsum lorem ipsum lorem ipsum lorem ipsum
lorem ipsum lorem ipsum lorem ipsum

Lorem ipsum lorem ipsum lorem ipsum lorem ipsum lorem ipsum
lorem ipsum lorem ipsum lorem ipsum lorem ipsum lorem ipsum lorem

Which of the two pages did you notice more? The totally unexpected pileup of letters, of course, because that graphic is different from every other page in this book. Your eyes and brain have become accustomed to seeing uniformly laid out letters and words on these pages (and indeed countless pages from countless other books), and it no longer takes much brain power to recognize what you're seeing. The image of the pileup, on the other hand, is totally new and therefore demands your brain's attention. If I inserted that same visual on every third page for the rest of the book, though, not only would you get used to seeing it and attend to it less, but in a few chapters you would also get so good at skipping over that page that soon you would barely notice that visual.

Vocal variety is the human communication animal consistently and frequently changing the sound of the voice so the listener will attend to what is being said...and then attend again...and again...and again. It's how we take advantage of our audience's need for novelty.

If you don't use vocal variety in high-stakes situations, you're fighting your audience's DNA.

WHAT IS IDEAL?

Disclaimer: All this is not to say that more vocal variety is always better. Taken too far, extreme vocal variety turns into chaos and makes comprehension difficult, even impossible. Early AI voice software sounded unnatural to listeners because the vocal variety seemed haphazard and extreme. If one put a five-minute pause in between words, one's listener would likely leave the room and probably the building. If you made the loudest sound you're capable of on one word and then the softest possible on the very next word, people wouldn't think you're a scintillating speaker, just a silly one.

There is in fact a sweet spot—an ideal range, if you will. You can't speak in a constant way that puts people to sleep; you also can't speak in a chaotic way that scares them. You must achieve coherence.

To help you understand that range of vocal variety, consider a bell curve with those three C words. If sounds are constant—enduring and unchanging—they become incoherent because eventually they don't even register to our awareness. Too much vocal variety, on the other hand, turns into chaos, and if taken to an absurd degree could even indicate that the speaker would be a safety risk. So a communicator must avoid the extremes of chaos and constancy at the two opposite ends of the curve and instead use vocal variety that achieves coherence.

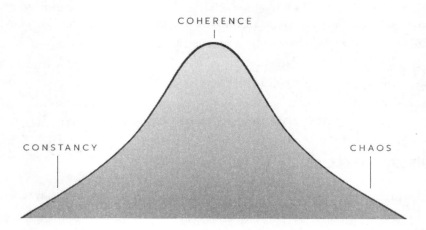

COHERENCE

CONSTANCY   CHAOS

That is a deeeeeeeep dive into vocal variety. But I wanted to give you a rigorous understanding of why using vocal variety is so important. Now here's the rub. When you get into higher-stakes communication situations, it is very likely that you shift to the left on the bell curve, coming perilously close to or even entering the constancy extreme. Why? Under stress, we cope by resorting to the classic three F strategies: fight, flight, or freeze. In a communication situation, fighting or flying are generally frowned upon, so the only option becomes freezing. No one wants to stand in front of an audience or meeting room and say absolutely nothing, so we do the second-best option: We freeze as much as we can. Think of a bunny rabbit freezing in front of the headlights of an oncoming car—the animal tries to make its visual profile small and still in hopes that it won't be noticed. Humans do a version of this—we try to make ourselves smaller, to contract as much as we can. But to speak is to move; we move our tongue and lips, our rib cage and diaphragm, our brow and face. So if speaking necessitates moving, we try to move less so we are noticed less. But this adaptation—though potentially effective with lions, tigers, and bears—doesn't help for speaking.

When I observe clients shrink their posture, restrain their gestures, limit their facial expressions, and—yes—reduce their vocal variety, I coach them with a simple phrase: "What you think is keeping you safe is actually putting you in danger." They are in more danger of bombing the interview, blowing the presentation, or messing up the meeting because they are contracting their communication instrument.

The goal is not to have unlimited vocal variety but rather to employ the same amount and range of vocal variety you would when at your most other-focused.

To unlock that same range, let's now get to the drills.

PRIMARY EXERCISE

The first point to make is that you have already built some skill in terms of vocal variety from using the last chapter's lesson. As I mentioned in its final paragraph, the cork exercise helps slow pace. And—because you just learned in this chapter that the Five Ps are interconnected—there is a very high likelihood the cork affected all your other Ps as well. So when it comes to vocal variety, you are already in a better position than before you read the last chapter! But let's supercharge that development.

As you do these exercises, don't worry about which words to emphasize. Concern yourself with *having* vocal variety, not where to use it.

To understand why I say this, consider an actor-training tool that pitches a parenthetical phrase differently from the rest of the thought. First it shifts it high; the second time, low. Actors study this technique so they can make long arcs of text clear to an audience. Try it quickly if you want. Say this sentence twice. The first time shift the parenthetical (the phrase inside the parentheses) to a significantly higher pitch than the first and last portions of the sentence. The second time do the opposite.

I'll show you what I mean by how I position the text on the page:

(which is more physical than you might think)

Spoken communication   ↑   ↑   ↑   ↑   ↑   is important.

Spoken communication   ↓   ↓   ↓   ↓   ↓   is important.

(which is more physical than you might think)

See how the meaning of the sentence is perfectly clear regardless of whether the parenthetical is set apart either high or low? The essential thing is that it is set apart and therefore indicates difference from the other parts of the sentence. In the case of parentheticals, that difference typically implies that the information, although additive, is not essential. But it doesn't matter if the shift goes high-low-high or low-high-low. It just matters that there is a shift. So don't overanalyze for which words or phrases you should most vary your voice; just vary your voice. Let's get to work doing just that now.

Silent Storytelling

Although it can be effortless to use vocal variety when you're not self-focused, the trick is to do so when you are. And that brings me to the primary kinesthetic activity for this chapter. Interestingly, the fastest way I've found to help someone vary their Ps is actually with a kinesthetic drill that at first appears to have nothing to do with your voice. It's called Silent Storytelling.

First Step: Record (Again, Please!)

In a moment, I want you to speak on any professional topic and use your smartphone to video record yourself. You need a topic you can speak about for at least five to ten minutes because we'll be starting and stopping within it multiple times.

Once you have a topic chosen, please video record yourself talking on the topic for roughly two minutes. When you've finished recording, please don't watch the video yet. And please don't delete the footage either. In fact, we're going to reference this footage again in future chapters, so if you can, please keep it. I promise the reveal will be worth it. Ready? Go record yourself, and then come right back.

* * *

Next, try Silent Storytelling.

In this drill, you are allowed to communicate to an audience using all of yourself *except* your voice. The idea is to use all your communication instrument as expressively as needed to help an audience understand precisely what you're saying, even without the benefit of the sound of your voice. Essentially, the activity is like very expressive lip-synching. You could also think of it like watching a very animated speaker on TV with the sound muted. To clarify, this is not charades; you do not need to "act out" the words. You are simply using more of your physical communication instrument—your face, lips, mouth, and hands—to ensure your message is received, even without sound. That means you will need to: (1) silently enunciate (in effect, lip-synch) your words so expressively that a listener might be able to read your lips; (2) gesture with sufficient expressiveness and specificity that a listener might understand where/when/who/how by watching the story your hands are telling; and (3) allow your facial expressions to vary and reflect the ups/downs, ins/outs, and lefts/rights of your content. Just think of this as turning up the volume on every aspect of your communication because you can't turn up the volume on the sound. Ready? I thought so! Try Silent Storytelling on the same topic now, either continuing from where you left off or repeating the same section, and record yourself as you do. Say your stuff, but with no sound.

(Please don't watch the video yet!)

* * *

View the Evidence: Now Watch Your Handiwork

Well done! Now you get to review the footage. First, quickly glance at the two clips. Were you doing the drill? If the footage from both looks identical—the same range of hand gestures, facial expressions, and enunciation, even though one has sound and one doesn't—that means you didn't go far enough with the drill. If that's the case, do the Silent Storytelling portion again, but this time push yourself to actually do the drill!

In the words of Spinal Tap, "Turn it up to eleven"—but an eleven of physical expressiveness, not sound. Once you've done that, watch again. If the two clips are still identical, do it again, but go further with expressiveness. You're not done until the two clips look quite different.

*   *   *

Now comes the fun part—you get a reprieve! You get to add sound back into the mix, but not all at once....

In a moment, you'll get an opportunity to practice Silent Storytelling again, but this time with an imaginary remote control. As you continue speaking your content and recording yourself, every so often you get to allow sound back into the equation. Roughly every fifteen to thirty seconds, I want you to alternate between using sound and not. Imagine you are a character in a television show, and a trigger-happy little kid is pressing the mute button on and off in a maddening manner. Allow yourself to do this exercise long enough to alternate between the two modes multiple times. Your job is devastatingly simple: You must keep the full range and expressivity of your facial expressions, gestures, and enunciation, whether you're allowing sound or not. Once completed, you should be able to watch the full clip on mute and not "know" when you were speaking silently. Ready? Do that final round of practice and recording now. (Please wait to watch the footage.)

*   *   *

And now the magic trick's great unveiling: watch the footage of the final clip and compare it to the first in this series. Notice the dramatic changes in terms of vocal variety—pace, pitch, pause, power, placement. Voilà!

What's going on here? Remember the phrase Ralph Zito taught me (Chapter 4, for those of you who like to read back): Your voice is your body. If you alter the physical communication instrument that is your body, the sound that instrument makes will change. If you're more physically expressive, you'll tend to be more vocally expressive too.

Surprisingly, this exercise for vocal variety takes the focus off your voice entirely, which, as your coach, is precisely what I'm trying to do to short-circuit some of the negative self-talk and thought-suppression traps I highlighted at the start of the chapter. But how can a drill with no focus on the voice yield vocal changes? The increased space in the back of the throat from having to mouth the words so specifically modifies the shape and size of the inside of the mouth and throat so your voice is more resonant (*placement*); the exaggerated time it takes to shape each word specifically forces you to slow down at times (*pace*); it takes time to think of what to say next because it feels terrible to silently mouth the word *um*, and that focus on linguistic precision increases thinking time between words or thoughts (*pause*); more physicality and gestures tend to lead to freer and fuller breathing, providing more fuel for melodic range (*pitch*); and all these changes—more space in the mouth, more enunciation, more time, more breath—contribute to an expanded range in volume (*power*).

Am I suggesting that you need to be more expressive with your face, mouth, and hands in your communication life? Perhaps. We'll explore that question in myriad ways throughout this book, and you will certainly come to some conclusion on that question by the end (if not much sooner). But regardless of whether you determine that you should be more expressive overall, what I can safely say right now is that if you know that monotone or lack of vocal variety is a challenge, the drill you just learned is one of the quickest ways to change your habit.

Silent Storytelling can be both a practice and a performance drill. Regarding the former, you just practiced it. Do so again—early and often. But you can also use this as a performance drill. Just challenge yourself to use more of your face, mouth, and hands while speaking, secure in knowing that if you do those things, your vocal variety will come along for the ride. Want a sly trick to remind yourself to do so? Start off video calls on mute; begin speaking in a physically expressive manner; soon would-be altruists on your call will remind you to unmute; at which point, do so, apologize, but go right on speaking for the remainder of your call with that heightened level of physical expressivity.

SECONDARY EXERCISES

Play Your Horn Hand

This next drill will give you the chance to channel your inner jazz musician and imitate the musical stylings of a New Orleans street performer improvising on their clarinet, trombone, or trumpet. I call it Play Your Horn Hand. It's simple.

In a moment I want you to use your hand like the mouthpiece of a horn or woodwind instrument. First, close your fingers into a fist with your thumb out to make a thumbs-up gesture. Next, put the tip of your thumb to your lips, and imagine your hand has become that clarinet, trombone, or trumpet. The next part is easy: hum. Without opening your lips, "play" your horn hand and see how much musical range you can use. Challenge yourself to hum through various runs of notes from high to low (pitch variation), loud to soft (power), short and long pauses (pause— which is a great time to breathe!), and fast and slow (pace). We'll not concern ourselves with placement for this exercise; it's partly dictated by the act of humming, so relieve yourself from having to account for it. In this exercise (and in life), breathe as much as you need to play your music with abandon.

For the musical selection, you can just improvise, à la a great jazz street performer. Make up a melody that encompasses a huge musical range. If that feels too amorphous, you can also use a melody you know. To get the juices flowing, consider any of the following or any other piece in the whole wide world that covers a large pitch range. (Note: My native language is English, so most of the following song references are US-centric English songs, but this exercise will work with any song in any language, so long as the song covers a large pitch range.)

+ "In the Mood" by the Glenn Miller Orchestra
+ "The Star-Spangled Banner" by Francis Scott Key
+ "Cancan" by Jacques Offenbach
+ "Don't Stop Me Now" by Queen
+ "Seven Nation Army" by the White Stripes
+ "Blues in the Night" by Harold Arlen
+ "Sir Duke" by Stevie Wonder
+ "Do Right Woman" by Aretha Franklin
+ "The Greatest Love of All" by Whitney Houston
+ "Roar" by Katy Perry

When you're ready and have made your musical choice, play! Use a bounteous amount of air and breathe in generously through the nose after extended phrases to gather your breath for the next run of notes. Make the tune ambitious and rangy—use that full scale! Can you encompass an octave and a half, or even two? Two and a half?

If you've not already tried it, do so now.

* * *

Good job!

Now that you've played your hand a bit, in a moment I want you to transition into speech. This time around, hum some more music into your hand, but then as soon as you've finished that chorus or sixteen bars or that verse, shift and try to match the range and variety you just did playing your "instrument" but while speaking the words of your content. If you'd like to give yourself a break from your professional subject matter, here are a couple additional topics (or you can just make up your own):

+ What is your favorite kind of music and why?
+ How does kinesthetic learning help you remember things?
+ What will be the future of reading?

When you speak, your job is to use as much variety as when you were playing the instrument. Ready? Go!

* * *

This drill is obviously for practice, not performance. It's also an excellent rapid-fire exercise you can use to warm up your vocal variety before going into communication situations.

Lego Drill for Vocal Variety

Did you achieve mastery yet with the Lego drill you learned in Chapter 6? I hope so, because you're going to do it again but this time to unlock vocal variety. If you have your Lego blocks handy, note whether they are different colors. Ideally, you have five or six different colored Lego blocks (red, blue, yellow—you get the drift). Now do the Lego drill again, but this time make each thought sound quite different from the others by unreservedly changing your vocal variety from thought to thought. So, if THOUGHT ONE SOUNDS LIKE THIS, thought two might sound like this, and *thought three could sound like this*, and so on. The different colored Lego blocks are your visual cue that each thought is unique and needs unique vocal variety, different from the previous and the following.

Please be mindful that blocks number one and number two are very frequently quite different, but blocks three, four, and five can tend to fall into the same pattern. Push yourself to go as far as possible through the entire series. You may feel like you have "run out" of options by the third or fourth sentence. That's okay. Persevere. I promise ingenuity will strike and you will find new options if you keep pushing yourself.

Substitutions for Colored Blocks

If you don't have different colored Lego blocks, you can modify the drill in two ways. One, if you have Lego blocks that are all the same color, stack them in a unique way each time—attached and shifted to the left, then shifted right, then fully overlapping on all the points of contact, and so forth. In this incarnation, the varied attachment is your reminder that each thought is unique, needs unique vocal variety, and needs to be different from the previous and the following thoughts. Two, if you are using single-color sticky notes, tear some into six different-sized pieces. Make one the full-sized untouched note; make another about two-thirds the size by ripping off a third of the paper; perhaps another can be a tiny fraction of an actual note—like one-twelfth of a sticky note. In this incarnation, the variously sized notes are your reminders that each thought is unique and needs unique vocal variety.

PRO TIP

If you want an instant way to see what your vocal variety "looks like," use the same tool I offered that politician and record yourself in the voice recorder app on your smartphone and try to do a "good" and "bad" version; then look at the visual representation of the sound. It will look something like this:

CHAPTER 9
VOCAL VARIETY

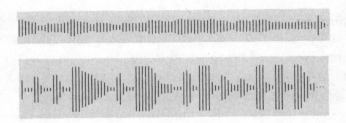

Play around with what it looks like when using more or less; tell a thrilling story versus a dry elevator pitch; see what "going too far" looks like; then listen back to "too far" and evaluate by what percentage too far it is (likely not as far as you thought when creating it). Please note that this exercise can only really give you data on pace, pause, and power. Technically, the visual representation can't indicate pitch or placement, but it's safe to assume that if you're varying the other three, pitch and placement will come along for the ride.

PRACTICE OR PERFORMANCE?

As I've mentioned for each, most of the drills in this chapter are for practice only. But you can use these drills for performance unaltered or slightly altered when...

WHAT ABOUT VIRTUAL?

...you're on video calls! Just as you can stack Lego blocks for conciseness, so can you stack variously colored Lego blocks for vocal variety under the boundary of the camera's frame. Additionally, just as you can watch for your enunciation by observing your own video box and watching real time to see if there is space between your top and bottom teeth, you can also observe your physical presence. Are you moving your brow, lips, and hands freely and expressively? It's safe to assume your vocal variety is also expressive. Are you restrained in all those behaviors? Then it's also safe to assume your vocal variety is restrained. So you can't silently tell stories, but you can watch for the same behaviors that Silent Storytelling unleashes and use the video to hold yourself accountable.

WRAPPING UP

I recognize I've offered a lot of drills for this topic. I did so for two purposes. First, I want you to have multiple ways to unlock this topic. Now you have that! But my second purpose is a bit sneakier: I want to desensitize you to the activity of listening to your voice. Did you notice yourself becoming at least 1 percent more of a scientist in this chapter? Perhaps you began to listen to the sounds you were making dispassionately, noticing the Five Ps more and your self-critique less?

Ideally, the answers to those questions are a resounding yes. Because giving your inner critic a rest is essential when we're talking about vocal variety.

It's particularly important because there are plenty of outer critics to contend with too. Let's talk about those critics in the next chapter.

CHAPTER 10

VOCAL CRITIQUES AND SEXISM

How to Deconstruct Problematic Feedback
(and Use More of Yourself)

Hopefully, you feel newly skilled and emboldened to set forth into a brave new world of vocal variety. And with that skill and boldness, hopefully you can be cajoled into examining one aspect of vocal-variety teaching that frustrates me. And if you have ever been the recipient of critiques about your vocal variety, I bet it frustrates you too.

We're going to explore two specific vocal-variety patterns: upspeak and vocal fry. We'll start with upspeak.

First, the word *upspeak* is a general term for a very specific vocal pattern (the technical term is high-rising terminal, as in the terminal—or last—sound rises). If you have never heard the term, you could be forgiven for thinking that upspeak might be anything from talking louder to emphasizing words on the first and third beats (that's a nod to you jazz fans out there) to a command for an AI voice assistant. Rather, it's the common term for a very specific habit of inflecting the voice up in pitch at the tail end of sentences and phrases.

In general, upspeak in English indicates continuation and it conveys one of three ideas:

1. I'm asking a question, and in order to continue this conversation, I need your answer.
2. I'm in the process of sharing several ideas and I'm going to continue with more information.
3. I'm defining a list and mentioning multiple things that fit together in some type of grouping that demands that I continue (a list of directions, for example).

But since upspeak technically doesn't have anything to do with your speech, I refer to it as upward inflection because that's slightly more accurate. But whatever you call it, the pattern has gotten a lot of attention in recent years. In particular, people have been fighting a bit of a culture war over it. Critics complain about how it sounds musically and what it conveys about the speaker; defenders point out that most of the critique is directed toward women, and particularly young women.

I am not—nor do I pretend to be—a gender, identity, diversity, equity, and inclusion expert. I can safely note that we (still) live in a sexist world; I can also safely note that not every critique of a female voice is necessarily sexist. But beyond that, I'm less interested in the question of "Is critiquing upward inflection a sexist activity?" and much more interested in how anyone, no matter who they are, can have more power to intentionally communicate the way they want.

It is undeniable that women have received a lot of absolutely garbage coaching about their voices through the ages. In previous eras, women were encouraged to speak in a light, high, and breathy manner to convey "femininity" (think of the voice Marilyn Monroe made famous in *Some Like It Hot*). But much of the current coaching women get now is also equally useless. Today's suggestions are costumed in the language of empowerment and career success: "Speak in the lower third of your voice because it conveys more authority"; "avoid upspeak because it sounds like you're asking for permission"; "pitch your voice deeper so people in the room take you more seriously." The idea, of course, is that these adjustments will supposedly help women advance in the business world. But it's not a far path to trace from today's "speak in the bottom third of your register" back to yesteryear's "don't speak in a shrill, high voice."

I have little patience for reductive coaching of any kind that aims to narrow the extent of what any given communicator can do. Should women speak in the lower register of their voices? Yes! Should they also speak in the middle and upper registers of their voices? *Yes!* Should they inflect downward at the ends of thoughts? Yes! But should they also inflect up at times, especially if they want to ask a question, convey that a thought is continuing, or vocally indicate that they're building a list? Of course!

And, importantly, if you have developed a style of speaking because of where you are from and who your community is that features frequent upward inflection, and that same ratio of upward inflection stays relatively constant whether you're talking to a friend in crisis or giving a Power-Point presentation, then let yourself off the hook! If you live in Ireland, for example, upward inflection would just be described as your dialect. No one would give you grief.

But let's say you have a very detail-oriented boss whose mission is to eradicate upward inflection or a performance review committee that has identified this as a communication habit you must transform in order to be considered for promotion. Then fine—let's examine ways to expand your speaking habits. But if that's the case, I encourage you to think of it with much more creativity, fun, and forgiveness than the subject is typically dealt with. You can even think of learning a new language, studying a dialect for a film role, or learning to inflect more like the people around you in a foreign country so that your speech is easier to comprehend to their ears. Then, like a scientist, see what you can discover by intentionally trying to end your sentences with as much finality as possible.

The problem is not upward inflection. Just as I've pointed out in other sections of this book, labeling something a problem and then fixating on that thing is a recipe for disaster—it activates all the traps of thought suppression.

So, let's not do that.

Instead, rather than a negative avoiding ("don't upward inflect"), shift the focus to a positive doing ("do end your sentences in varied ways to keep gauging and engaging your audience's interest"). In other words, instead of focusing on not ending your sentences inflecting up, let's focus on all the variety of ways you can end a sentence to try to achieve your goal.

Upward inflection is not the only vocal pattern that gets critiqued. Let's shift to vocal fry.

In its simplest, laymen-terms explanation, vocal fry is speaking without sufficient breath support and allowing the sound of the voice to amplify primarily in the throat. The meager amount of air flowing past the vocal cords creates a sound like a gravelly rumble. Think of a car inching forward in fits and starts as it runs out of gas.

Fry tends to happen at the ends of thoughts/sentences, and this is for a very logical reason: speaking uses air, and the longer one speaks without breathing again, the more likely it is one will run short.

Vocal fry regularly gets tumbled into a food fight of reductive pro/con critiques that occupy only the two most extreme ends of the spectrum: (1) vocal fry is an innate personal characteristic and any critique is a biased attack and may in fact be sexist; and (2) vocal fry is a nails-on-the-chalkboard career-ender and indicates lack of promotion potential.

Let me offer a more nuanced and liberating view. Vocal fry is a problematic habit—not because it's a sexist critique nor because it means your career will stall—but because it results from a speaker using less of themselves to communicate, in this case less breath.

Air is totally free. It's there for you, anytime you want it! If you feel like it, even now experience the freedom of indulging in all the air you want. Breathe in as fully and freely as you're able and say, "Air is free!" (And if "breathing in fully and freely" is challenging, never fear—breath is the subject of the very next chapter.)

The next time you feel yourself sliding into a pattern of vocal fry, rather than allowing that to trigger either negative self-talk or righteous defensiveness, consider that you have unrestricted access to as much air as you can possibly use, at any and every time you want it.

Even that thought may provide some breath-of-fresh-air perspective (no pun intended). If it does for you, you are definitively not alone. My company sends out an email newsletter every so often. Among all the newsletters we have ever sent out, the one focused on vocal fry garnered by far the most response. The gist of its content I have just shared in this chapter (if you want to read that original news-letter piece, feel free to scan the QR code).

I mention it because our tribe wrote back to us in droves, sharing comments like the fol-lowing. I think this email from a learning and development professional reveals why the piece hit a chord (the italics are my own).

> "I really liked this—both as someone who
> has struggled with vocal fry as a result of nerves, and as some-one who coaches and appreciates how much more impactful this message is when we *disassociate vocal fry from shame and unworthiness!*"

If you are concerned about your own habits with vocal fry, hopefully this chapter can give you, too, some tools to disassociate it from any emo-tional charge it has accrued—shame, unworthiness, or other.

Speaking of tools, let's get to exploring the kinesthetic ones to develop agility around vocal fry and upward inflection. Even if you don't speak with habitual upward inflection or vocal fry, you'll derive benefit from these drills. They unlock their own virtuous cycle because their core prin-ciple is an essential one:

FINISH YOUR THOUGHT.

If you learn to end your thoughts—where upward inflection and vocal fry typically occur—with more finality, what else might unlock? You may take more time to consider your next thought, thereby improv-ing your content; you may realize you don't need to continue after the third or fourth point, thereby making your content more concise; you may breathe more to have ample air to reach the end of the sentence, thereby improving the Five Ps of Vocal Variety and benefiting from all the positive effects of breath. I could continue.

BALL THROWING

In a moment I'm going to ask you to find or make a ball. How, you might ask? If you have any type of athletic ball near you, it will do—just make sure it's not so hard as to be dangerous, like a golf or baseball. A Wiffle, tennis, juggling, or foam ball—as well as many others—will do nicely. If you have a ball accessible, go grab it now.

Let's say you are in a ball-scarce location; never fear! Yet again you get to deface this venerable book. The next page is intended to be torn out and crumpled into an impromptu ball. It'll do for this exercise in lieu of a proper ball.

Once you have procured your ball (either paper or athletic), I'm going to ask you to speak on some content once again, but this time at the end of every single sentence you're going to throw the ball emphatically. Different from the Lego drill you learned in Chapter 6, this intervention (the throw) doesn't happen after completion of the thought but rather aligned exactly with the final word of the sentence. To be absolutely clear, you should be throwing the ball and saying the final word simultaneously. Your job as the speaker is to see what benefit unlocks from allowing your physical communication instrument to force you to finish your thought with gusto. If you are specifically trying to develop agility around upward inflection, adjust the target of your throw: Aim the ball down. Throw it straight into the floor.

Once you've done that first throw, continue speaking your content, but instead of throwing an actual ball, you can shift the exercise to throwing an imaginary "energy ball" so you don't need to have more than one ball. That's not to dissuade those of you who have many balls lying around. If you want to gather three, five, or more, go for it! But what matters most is not the ball you're using, but how the specific and emphatic throwing motion forces you to end your sentence with more finality than you might normally.

Please try the exercise now.

**BLANK PAGE FOR YOU TO RIP OUT AND
CRUMPLE UP INTO A PAPER BALL!**

(C'mon, you know you want to!)

Once you've mastered this drill, it's quite seamless to adjust it to a totally imperceptible activity: perhaps tapping a finger subtly or pushing down your toe deliberately.

STICKY NOTE DRILL FOR DOWNWARD INFLECTION

This exercise is a modification of the Lego/sticky note drill you learned in Chapter 6. But if that version of the exercise focused on placing the object after the end of the sentence, like the ball throwing you just practiced, this version shifts that placement one beat earlier to the final word. Here are the instructions in a single-sentence summary: pick up a sticky note before you begin speaking at the start of a thought; hold the note in the air as you share your thought; as you say the final word of the thought, place the note down; and adhere it to the table/desk/surface.

With the same level of discipline you hopefully just brought to ball throwing, try the sticky note drill now.

* * *

For both the ball-throwing and sticky note drills for downward inflection, the essential activity is bringing attention to the final word in the sentence. That is the fulcrum at which upward inflection happens. As you develop some agility with how you complete thoughts, you will discover that—just like last chapter's multiple punctuation marks that communicate a pause—you have other options besides just downward and upward inflection.

CONTINUATION DRILL

This is a drill I learned from Shane Ann Younts, a wonderful voice and speech teacher at the NYU Graduate Acting Program. It's an elegantly simple way to avoid vocal fry (and often upward inflection as well) by tricking your brain to move the finish line of a given thought. All it entails is this: Add the words "and I have more to say" to the end of each thought. By doing this, the pattern of upward inflection or vocal fry gets moved from the end of your actual thought to the six extra words you have just added. Since vocal fry and upward inflection usually happen at the ends of thoughts, extending where the "end" is shifts the pattern. Once you've become skilled with this exercise, experiment with removing the six additional words, but say them silently in your head.

PRACTICE OR PERFORMANCE?

The sticky note and ball-throw drills can be both practice and performance exercises. At first, practice solo to build muscle memory. Once you have, you can do them explicitly on . . .

WHAT ABOUT VIRTUAL?

. . . video calls. Modify the ball throw into a subtle physical gesture or adhere the sticky note quietly and imperceptibly below the camera's frame. Once you have the hang of it, you can even translate the drills into an imperceptible physical gesture you can use when live or remote.

As for the continuation drill, although you could probably get away with saying those additional words once in a meeting without anyone really taking note, if you did it after every thought—as the drill is designed—your listeners might become distracted and mystified by your verbal tic.

But you should practice, practice, practice it if you want to explore greater agility around vocal fry. Why? It forces your body to breathe ever so slightly more—whatever amount you need to speak six more words. And breath is the answer to vocal fry. It's the answer to a lot more than that actually. Which means we should probably get into it next. Take a deep breath, and turn the page.

CHAPTER 11

BREATHING

How to Put Air into Action (and Prevent Vocal Quiver)

Put air into action.

I hope you like those words. I do. The sharp attack of the *p*, the assonant *a*'s, the simplicity of the four-word manifesto. The poetry of it feels inspiring to me.

I'll explain more about why I like those words and hope you do, too, in a moment, but first let me contrast them with a word you might not like:

BREATHE.

Huh? Who would possibly dislike the word *breathe*?
I would.

Because in over a decade working with clients, as soon as you tell someone to breathe, one of three things happen:

1. They slip into a negative feedback loop of self-criticism in which they berate themselves for being bad at what is ultimately the simplest thing in the whole world. "I'm such a

nincompoop! Why do I need to be reminded to do the thing that is literally mandatory for staying alive?! What a dunce I am."

2. They immediately do a reset or stress-relief breath in which they breathe all the way in and all the way out. This breath has utility for releasing tension, anxiety, and stress, but it isn't all that useful in creating communication.

3. They strive for a general "feeling of Zen." This may be good for their health but, again, doesn't necessarily improve their communication.

None of the aforementioned three things are where I want their attention. Where do I want it? On the activity of using their breath to accomplish something, namely, forming words to reach a listener.

PUT AIR INTO ACTION.

The word *breathe* is itself part of the problem. It is a single-word command that is entirely self-focused with no explicit purpose. Who should breathe? Youyouyouyouyouyouyou, of course (who is *not* currently breathing). For what purpose? Not sure—perhaps just because it's a good idea?

Communication is not about you and your breath; it's about how you use your breath to reach your audience! Which is why I prefer∴

PUT AIR INTO ACTION.

That's what breath is for when it comes to communication. And when I tell clients they're going to learn to "put air into action," they instantly have more curiosity and less self-criticism.

I follow that phrase with another alliterative one: "You have baggage about your breath."

You probably have baggage about your breath too. You might think you don't; you probably do. Most of us do. It's for varied and sundry reasons, but it's hard to make it to puberty, never mind adulthood, without having some fairly monumental disruption of our natural breathing mechanism.

We learn to clench our jaw to prevent an outburst of emotion, to hold our tummies in to maintain a slimmer silhouette, to breathe shallowly into our chests since our diaphragms and bellies are compressed in chairs.

Those are just three of the most common maladjustments.

So, in this chapter, we'll explore breathing. But I encourage you to continually come back to that one concept: it's not just breathing for the sake of breathing; it's for the purpose of putting air into action.

Before we go any further, let's take a moment just to appreciate the very activity of breathing itself. It's a shame we have all that baggage, because breath is miraculous.

On the most basic level, your breath is keeping you alive. Right now. You need food, water, and shelter, of course, but more immediately than all that, you need oxygen!

And the act of breathing is literally a communion with the rest of the biosphere! In that astonishing moment of gaseous exchange that occurs in your alveoli, CO_2 is exchanged for O. You are actually taking the planet's molecules into your body and trading others back. In fact, take a breath right now. Inhale and exhale. I'll wait.

You just chemically interacted with the atmosphere!

Even more miraculous, that interaction can be voluntary or involuntary. Want to intentionally take a deep breath to inflate your lungs and prepare for a plunge into a pool? You can do it.

Want to take a nap by that pool? Your breath will keep right on trucking, your involuntary response continuing respiration, providing your organs the oxygen they need.

And, by the way (and most applicable to this book), it is what makes spoken communication even possible. Your breath is the fuel with which you can create sound and then words and then ideas. It is the water in the stream, the fire under the hot-air balloon, the gas (or battery) in the car.

But if breath is so miraculous, why isn't it the subject of the first chapter in this book or at least before the chapter on vocal fry?

Part of having baggage means that it can be challenging to unpack. So, instead, I like to give people early wins using kinesthetic training in other components of communication and then add breath once people are already cruising along on the communication-improvement superhighway.

To be clear, I could write an entire book just on breath. This chapter really just scratches the surface. But it's a good scratch, so even if you don't embrace the full journey of regaining a more organic connection to your breath, this chapter will help you take some very powerful first steps.

HOW BREATH WORKS

Why is breath important? I recognize that you know the obvious answer. On the most primal level, we need oxygen to live. But why is it important for communication?

It might sound like an obvious question—you know you should breathe more and better and easier and all the other adjustments, but why? Why is it so essential that you reconnect with your breath in as deep and free a way as possible?

As a communicator, you are basically a woodwind instrument, like a clarinet: Air flows over a vibration source, and that vibration source gets amplified and altered. For a clarinet, the source of that air is the player's lungs, the vibration source is the reed, and the amplification mechanism is the long cylinder of the tube and the open mouth at its end. For you, the source of the air is the lungs, the vibration source is your vocal cords, and the amplification mechanism is all the resonant chambers of your body, including your mouth, throat, sinuses, head, and chest. To feel the vibration created by the reed in your body, just place your hand on your throat and hum. Do you feel that gentle vibration? See—you are a clarinet.

The clarinet sounds best when the player feeds sufficient air through the instrument in a sustained manner.

You sound best when you do that too.

But don't just take my word for it; let's test. In a moment, I want you to expel all the air from your lungs and once they are completely evacuated, talk. That's right. Talk with virtually no air. I don't care what you talk about, so choose any content in the whole wide world.

Get ready to blow out all your air. Do it on a sustained *s* sound so it sounds almost like letting all the air out of a tire. Keep going past the point that feels comfortable. Then—without inadvertently reinflating your lungs or sipping in a tiny portion of air—talk. Ready to do that? Go! Expel all your air and then talk. Do it now.

* * *

Hopefully, you didn't faint or get so lightheaded you had to lie down.

Notice what that was like.

Now you get to do the opposite. You get to indulge in a bountiful, ample, voluminous amount of air and then talk. You can speak the same exact content or something different—I don't care in the slightest. This time take a nice, full, expansive breath, and then when you have that air in your lungs, talk.

* * *

What did you notice this time? Most immediately you probably noticed that it was simply harder to talk without breath. But go a layer deeper. Remember the Five Ps of Vocal Variety? Note how you were far more able to use those Five Ps in version two than in version one?

Air is the fuel that makes those Five Ps possible. The quality of sound and amount of variation in our voices dramatically impact our audience's impression of our presence.

What about your inner experience of panic or ease? When you speak with no breath—as you did in the previous exercise—your brain gets a terrified message from the cells of your body, which are essentially screaming, "We're drowning! BREATHE!" If you know you're someone who holds their breath or breathes too infrequently when presenting, part of the panic and unease you experience is simple survival—your body is going into an adrenaline response because it feels as though it is literally drowning, even though it's not.

What about the cogency of ideas you shared? Did you say dumber stuff in version one? Quiz from the introduction: What two things does your brain need to think of smart stuff? Remember? Time and oxygen. The first version of this exercise removes the latter.

What about any physical discomfort in version one? That's because speaking like that is the equivalent of running an engine without any oil.

Air allows your vocal folds to vibrate and flutter and hum like a fine-tuned machine. Air, in this case, is the lubricant that allows beautiful music to be made. If you take away the air—and that lubricant—the engine grinds its gears away mercilessly. In fact you can probably hear that grinding in your voice. Version one probably had more gravel and rasp. Remember our discussion of vocal fry in Chapter 10? This exercise forces vocal fry. If you speak without sufficient air too much of the time, just like an engine that breaks down without oil to lubricate its parts, your voice will break down too. When that happens, speakers and singers can develop vocal nodes.

Breath isn't just for meditation or survival. You can't make the music of your communication without it.

And the best way to get a sufficient amount of air is to allow your body to breathe as it prefers to—which is diaphragmatically. You probably have a pretty good idea of what diaphragmatic breathing is, but it's unlikely you do it sufficiently when you communicate. You did when you were six months old though—trust me. If you need a reminder, look at two pictures of my daughter when she was that age. I took a video of her when she was napping because even I couldn't believe how freely and expansively her tummy moved when she breathed. These two images are from the video—the one on the left is after she breathed out; the right, after she breathed in. Notice that her shoulders and chest are completely unmoved, but the belly is gently expanded in the second photo.

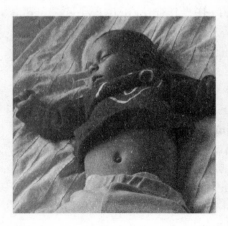 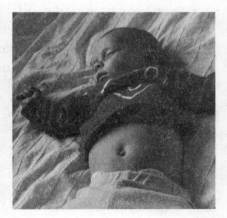

Diaphragmatic breathing demands that your diaphragm has suffi-cient room and relaxation to move up and down in your torso. The dia-phragm's rest position is actually up, sort of like the arch of a rainbow. It drops down when you take in a large breath and then reverts to its up or "rest" position as air leaves your body. If you chronically slump, you can understand why your diaphragm can't do its thing—it doesn't have enough room.

WHEN TO BREATHE

When should you breathe? This might sound like an absurd question, but it's worth being explicit about because I assure you many people have challenges "timing" their breathing and speaking.

(Note: In this chapter I'm talking about the in-the-moment activity of breathing while speaking. Breath is also a powerful tool for relaxation and centering before high-pressure situations, but I'll cover that in detail in Chapters 17 and 18.)

So, what is the answer to the question, When should you breathe? Whenever you want! As often as you want! Breath is one of the only things in this life that's still free. Use as much as you like!

Speakers can get hung up focusing on breathing at some mythical ideal juncture to convey gravitas or correlate their breathing to the punc-tuation of their thoughts.

This is not necessary. Consider that friend-in-crisis thought exper-iment we always use as our comparison; in that situation, you would breathe whenever necessary to share the flow of ideas you wanted.

Professional singers need to be disciplined about when to breathe; you don't. Even if you happen to be a professional singer, this book is about speaking well, not singing, so you, too, are off the hook. Singers often score a script and deliberately choose how they're going to phrase a line of singing. But that's because they must achieve a quite remarkable feat of enunciating words at a certain pitch level in a sustained manner on a very challenging scaffolding of sounds and words organized to music.

You just have to speak. So breathe—whenever you want, as much as you want. There is a secondary question though: When should you speak? I don't mean that as a question about "speaking up" or timing interjections; I mean within the breath cycle.

You might notice as you go through the exercises in this chapter that it's relatively easy to allow more breath to come into the body but that using that much breath to say words feels strange. This is a normal stage when you're learning to use breath more freely and expressively. Most likely it feels strange simply because you're used to speaking with far less air. Changing that habit and experimenting with using more will feel a bit foreign at first. Because it feels foreign, you're likely to try to cheat in one specific way: You'll probably waste the air of your more generous breaths by exhaling much of it before you begin making sound. You can think of that like a reset breath that features a big breath in, and then an equally large exhale.

That is not putting air into action. That is releasing air for relaxation. So just to make sure you understand the process of what to do with all the bountiful air you're going to learn to inhale in this chapter, let's learn to speak at the "top of the breath."

Referencing again the world of performance, *top of the breath* is a term singers use to describe the maximum inflation moment within the breath cycle. In other words, the moment to begin singing is when you have the full quantity of your inhale inside your lungs, not a few moments later when you have squandered a portion of the air. The aim is to start singing at the top of the breath.

So, too, should be the aim for speaking. To feel what I'm talking about, I want you to do two quick exercises.

The first is called a Yawn-Sigh, and once again it's a tool from theatrical and vocal performance. It's incredibly simple: Yawn, and when you have the maximum amount of air in your lungs, release the air on a long, sustained open vowel sound. You know how to do this because you've done it before in your life. See yourself on a lazy weekend morning, stretching luxuriously, the stretch triggering a yawn, and then—like a kingly lion on the plains of the Serengeti—hear yourself releasing a groan or vocal sigh. This is that same thing, only you must start making the vocal sigh as soon as you begin releasing air, and you must sustain it all the way until you've completed your full exhale. Also, remember the Five

Ps of Vocal Variety? Try to go from a high pitch to a lower one while you do the Yawn-Sigh exercise. Try it now.

* * *

That's a Yawn-Sigh, but you can't sigh your way through life. You have to say words, not just sounds. So next I'm going to prove to you that you already know how to put air into action at the top of the breath.

We're going to sing.

Don't panic. You already know the song.

In a moment, adjust your physical surroundings in such a way that you can sing the song "Happy Birthday" in a big, full-throated way. Please indulge in abundant air as you sing. Then, pay attention to what you do in the musical rest between the second and third stanzas of the song. Sing it now!

* * *

What did you do? If you're like most folks, you took a large breath in between the second and third stanzas, and then used that air right away at the top of the breath to give a crescendo to the final chorus.

So, (1) breathe as often as you need, and (2) speak at the top of the breath.

Now you know, but it's not enough to know; we have to shift the knowing into doing. Which brings us to the how.

HOW TO BREATHE

First, let me remind you of an insight from Chapter 2: You already know how to do this! No one needs coaching on diaphragmatic breathing to shout "Stop!" when a child runs into a busy street. In that moment your instinctual communication instrument takes over and the word bursts right out of your mouth.

The trick is unlocking what you can do then, but doing so in more cerebral and less instinctual situations—some of which might present zero consequences for a child pedestrian but potentially massive consequences for your career.

At some point you've probably had someone counsel you to breathe diaphragmatically and test whether you're doing so by telling you to put your hand on your tummy and check if it protrudes and then pulls back in. The reason that tummy action happens is because, when your diaphragm moves down and your lungs fill with air, the rest of your internal organs need to find somewhere to go to make room for the lungs. So they get pushed down and away, hence the feeling of the tummy pushing out.

I'll offer a more subtle way to feel diaphragmatic breathing. Place your hands on your "back side ribs." Use the same hand on the same side. For example, place the palm of your right hand on your right ribs as far to the back as you can reach. With your hand placed there, take as deep a breath as you can and see if you can note the expansion of your ribs.

Keep your hand there and breathe a bit. Notice how the whole torso expands as you fill with air—your hand might feel the slight sensation of being pushed back in space. You may even feel a tiny increase in the space in between each rib. Your rib cage is not one bone; it is many bones, all connected by cartilage and sinew and muscle. The points at which the ribs connect with your spine are in fact joints; those joints can move—a little. And when you breathe in the manner I'm describing, you'll become more and more aware of the movement in all the bones of your torso.

Now that you've felt that, try to maintain it but with even more subtle physical feedback. Please find somewhere to sit in which your back is supported by a firm structure: A standard chair is fine. I want you to breathe diaphragmatically again. This time, see if you can still feel the sensation of your back side ribs expanding ever so slightly into the back of that support structure. This is a useful thing to practice; if you are doing it well—and can actually feel the subtle movement—you are breathing in a deep, diaphragmatic way. Also, you can do it anytime, anywhere (provided you're seated) and no one can see that you are working on your breathing.

If you want an image, imagine that when you breathe in, your lungs are filling with air from the bottom up, as a balloon does when it's filled with water from the spigot of a sink.

That's diaphragmatic breathing.

But that's all well and good when you have minutes to sit and focus on each and every single breath. How the heck do you take that type of breathing and actually use it to speak? To put air into action, let's do three fun exercises. They each teach the same thing, but different ones resonate with different people, so feel free to hang on to the one you like the best. Each of these will require that you use more air and put that air into action. We do these because the problem that most adults in the modern world experience with their breathing is that they subsist and speak with too little breath. The rare person overuses their breath and habitually hyperventilates, but they are the exception and in those cases the problem is not so much that they're speaking with too much air but rather they are taking in and releasing large amounts while not actually using it to form words. For the lion's share of people, the main task is to use more air. So that's where we'll focus.

Exercise 1: Play Your Horn Hand for Breath

In a moment I want you to play your hand again, but this time focus on breath rather than vocal variety. Instead of making a thumbs-up gesture, close your fingers into a fist, but retain a bit of space between your curled fingers and your palm so a stream of air can flow through that channel.

When you're ready, I want you to "play" a bit of music by blowing the melody through that channel. For the musical selection, you can use the same song you used before or try something new. When you "play," use the sound of the letter *d* followed by any vowel sound that feels easy so your music will essentially sound like a series of *doo-doo-doo-doo* notes, not dissimilar to the sound of a kazoo. Work hard to get plenty of sound out the far end of the musical instrument mouthpiece (your hand). (Helpful hint: If you go far enough with this, the vibration of the *doo-doo-doo* sounds will create a buzz in your hand.)

Try that for a few moments. Play your hand with as much flair as you can!

*   *   *

Well done!

In a moment I want you to transition into speech. This time around, play some more music into your hand, but in short order shift to speech and use that same amount of breath power to support your words as was previously supporting your music.

Ready? Go!

* * *

Nice job.

Were you able to use more breath to speak? Good!

Why does this exercise work? In essence, your hand has extended the length of your body's musical instrument; instead of traveling only from your larynx to your lips to exit your body, sound now must travel some inches farther (depending on the size of your hand), and your body automatically marshals more breath to cover that added distance. Then when you take that hand away, your body has become accustomed to using more air and so it carries over into the act of speaking too.

Like the Play Your Horn Hand exercise for vocal variety, this is a practice drill as well as an excellent warm-up exercise right before larger communication situations.

Exercise 2: Blow Up a Balloon

If you've not been able to get in the groove of the Horn Hand exercises, this drill can achieve the same outcomes but without requiring that you embrace your inner musician. Instead, all you must do is blow up a balloon. If for some reason you actually have a balloon accessible, by all means take a moment and go get it! I'll wait....

For everyone else who lacks a balloon, you can do the drill by simply imagining one. Use the first three fingers of each hand to place a pretend balloon in front of your lips and prepare to inflate it. Steady your hands so air doesn't slip out the sides of the balloon's opening; when you're ready, use a consistent and strong flow of air to fight past the initial tightness of the unstretched balloon. Blow all your air into the balloon; once you've come to the end of your breath, keep the pretend balloon in place, breathe in a huge breath through your nose—all while keeping the balloon in position. Then when your lungs are full again, drive that slow, steady stream of air into the balloon again. If you haven't already tried this exercise, do it now.

When you do this a couple times, I promise you'll tap back into the muscle memory of how much lung power it takes to blow up a party balloon. Remember that experience? It takes more than one lungful to get enough air into the balloon to make an awesome party. At the end of each breath, one must keep the balloon pressed against the embouchure (Merriam-Webster's: "the position and use of the lips, tongue, and teeth in playing a wind instrument") and pull in a large amount of air through the nose to gather enough fuel to inflate the balloon more.

Once you really feel the experience of using your full lung power to inflate a huge party balloon, transfer that same experience to speaking and try to use that same amount of breath. Here are some new topics you can speak on, or you can refer to the previous exercise and choose a topic you didn't use last time (or—again—make up your own):

- What was the best party with balloons you ever attended?
- Discuss how muscle memory works.
- Share a professional success story.
- Describe someone you admire as a leader.
- Share some of the progress in your communication since beginning this book.

When you speak, your job is to use as much breath as when you were inflating the party balloon. Ready? Go!

* * *

Did you use more breath to speak? Good!

Why does this exercise work? It forces you to experience just how expanded your lungs can be, and it taps into an activity we've all done—and one that hopefully has some positive associations for you.

Exercise 3: Drag on a "Cigarette"

I tread into the following terrain very cautiously: This next exercise relies on pretending to inhale a deep drag on a cigarette. To be exceptionally clear: I do not recommend you smoke! And if this exercise would in any way trigger a desire to smoke again if you are a former smoker or a craving if you are currently trying to quit, by all means don't do the drill! The only reason I include it here is it's such an immediate way to realize just how little we typically breathe and just how much we actually can. With that giant disclaimer complete, please proceed at your own risk. Here is the exercise.

To make the experience more realistic, you will see a blank square on the next page, roughly the size of a cigarette rolling paper. So, if you like creative simulation, you get to tear out a page of this book yet again. Go ahead—tear the following page out!

Now roll that paper into the basic size and shape of a cigarette. You now get to portray your best 1950s beatnik hanging out in a smoky coffee shop. I want you to pretend you're taking a deep and long drag off a cigarette. See how much "smoke" you can take into your lungs.

With this drill, you can move into speaking much more quickly. I want you to hold court on some highly erudite subject, profound topic, or existential question. Your job is to take a huge drag on your cigarette, and then share a thought or two. Then another huge drag, another thought or two. Continue doing this until you really feel the vast amount of air you can—but very likely don't—use when you typically speak.

Here are some fun topics to choose from:

+ What is the meaning of life?
+ Which came first: chicken or egg?
+ What is the nature of enlightenment?
+ What lies beyond infinity?

(Surgeon Author's warning: This paper is to be used only for improving one's communication skills by imitating the activity of taking a long drag on a cigarette. **Smoking cigarettes is bad for your health. Improving your communication is good for it!)**

CUT HERE.
FOLLOW THE
DASHED LINES.

PRACTICE OR PERFORMANCE?

Both the balloon and the cigarette drills can be used for practice and performance. You just did the practice. For performance situations, remove the prop (real or imaginary) from the equation, but rely on the muscle memory you have built from the exercise. Retain the size and depth of your breath and use all that fuel to power your words, or to put air into action.

WHAT ABOUT VIRTUAL?

It's silly to say breath applies to virtual situations, too, because it's so obvious. Moreover, where does breath not apply? It's a necessary precondition for pretty much everything.

But it is worth making one point about breath when virtual, which is this: Pay attention to how you do or do not contort your body when on phone or video calls. We'll explore this further in the chapters on posture and stance, but constricting and contorting your body also constricts and contorts the airway to breathe. So if you habitually hold your phone by pinning your ear to your shoulder or you chronically crane your head forward and down to get closer to your computer's camera and microphone, remind yourself of this hierarchy: Technology is there to support you; you are not there to support technology. Consider the ramifications of your physical habits and patterns when working remotely and see whether you can improve how you use breath in those situations too.

Of all the chapters in this book, the subject matter you just learned is both the easiest and the hardest to integrate. Why? Because you have literally limitless moments to practice every single day. Any time you take a breath, you can be putting what you've learned in this chapter into practice. But that's also the hard part, because having unlimited opportunities invites both overload and procrastination. It's too much to practice all the time, and you can always "get to it tomorrow."

I challenge you to avoid these pitfalls. Bring some focus to your breath each day. I promise you it will be time and attention well spent.

Consistency matters more than intensity. Ten minutes every day is better than ten consecutive hours every six months.

Speaking of which, why not take ten minutes and do some of the exercises you just learned in this chapter? And when you come back, we're going to look at where you look. Eye contact is next.

CHAPTER 12

EYE CONTACT

How to Focus on Your Audience (and Not Your Eye Contact)

We now come to one of the trickiest aspects of communication training that should actually be the simplest: eye contact.

Why is it tricky? Because all too frequently people think of and treat eye contact as something they either "have" or don't. You'll hear presenters seek feedback after an event by asking, "How was my eye contact?" as though eye contact was part of their wardrobe.

The phrase *eye contact* is deeply misleading because it is a compound noun for what ultimately should be a verb. The title of the skill should be "focus on the other person," "look at your listener," "note whether your audience is following you"—or some other action-verb phrase that conveys a fluid, ongoing process rather than a solid state.

I recognize that might seem like an overly semantic deconstruction of the term, but it's important. Because framing eye contact as Eye Contact reinforces the fallacy that eye contact is about the person doing the speaking; great eye contact is about the person you're speaking to.

Still, I am going to continue to refer to this subject with the term *eye contact*—not because I think it's accurate but because it's ubiquitous. To help you remember that eye contact is not a static attribute but a dynamic process, I'm going to share this hand-scrawled illustration of the words written into a smiley face to give you a (slightly ridiculous) reminder that eye contact is about focusing on them, not you.

To begin, a caveat: Nowhere in this chapter—or in this book—do I wade into the territory of cultural differences about eye contact. Different cultures and societies have different norms for eye contact, informed by situation, status, familiarity, formality, decorum, and many other nouns that demarcate the endless complexity and nuance of human interactions. If you want precise ratios about how much eye contact to use when receiving communion, being crowned monarch of a nation, or enjoying tea at a formal ceremony, this book won't help you. If, on the other hand, you want to learn the skill of being intentional with your eye contact so you can make whatever decision you want regarding it in all those various and specific situations, read on! Once you have built your skills, you can better navigate the varying norms and expectations of global audiences because you'll have mastery over your physical communication instrument.

On the most fundamental level, eye contact comes from a speaker's deep primal need to see whether they've been understood and a listener's deep primal need to assure the speaker that they have been. No caveperson ever said to another caveperson, "There's a saber-toothed tiger over there," with bad eye contact.

This is why the output-based coaching I mentioned in earlier chapters is so bogus. Instructions like "hold eye contact for the length of one thought" or "hold eye contact for eight to twelve seconds" are utterly arbitrary.

So, rather than envisioning good eye contact as something one does or does not *have*, I invite you to think of good eye contact as a result of being authentically focused on the other person.

And what about when there are many other persons? Speakers often ask me questions like: "Where should I look when giving a presentation to a large group of people?" "Should I scan the room?" "Should I look above everyone's heads?" "Should I divide the room roughly into four quadrants and make sure I look to each one?" At this point in the book, you can probably imagine how I might critique that last question: It's arbitrary. Why 4 quadrants? Why not 7 or 16.3? And what about the people who are on the fringes of those quadrants? Which quadrant do they go in—quadrant 2 or 3?

The best practice when speaking to a large audience is essentially the same process as talking to one person: Focus on reaching individuals in the audience. Once you've gotten some sort of reaction or acknowledgment of comprehension from one set of eyes, move on to another. And then, yes, you can force yourself to move around to various portions of the room and audience, but the activity is still the same—look into the individual eyeballs of your listeners to gauge whether they're comprehending what you're sharing.

To test this, again imagine yourself in a highly other-focused group situation. Envision yourself giving a rah-rah pep talk between innings to a Little League team. Imagine yourself looking into the eyes of each kid to see who is going to need some cheering up, who will be a quick convert and a rallying force for the other kids, and who will need both a carrot and a stick.

The performing artists who can command an entire room, hall, or amphitheater are masters at this. The more you make any given person in an audience feel heard and felt and listened to by maintaining eye contact with them, the more you have an opportunity to make all their buddies around them feel that way as well. Get in the habit—even at large speaking engagements—of making eye contact with individual people.

This might sound simple enough when you're engrossed in the situation. The challenge is when you're not engrossed. The challenge is also when you're not eager for the directness and interpersonal connection that can blossom when two people look each other in the eyes.

Because of the power of eye contact in communication (and potential discomfort with that power), many of the people I have coached defend their lack of consistent eye contact. They'll say: "I don't want to be too intense [or too direct or too confrontational] with my eye contact because I don't want to make people uncomfortable." In nearly twenty years in professional communication training, what I have found is that most of the people who think they make too much eye contact make too little. So if you can envision that objection coming out of your mouth, I invite you to try on this idea. All those concerns are in fact much less likely than what your listener actually experiences: the feelings of not being paid attention to, not being heard, and not being valued.

Along with concerns about being overly direct or intense, one of the other primary ways people talk themselves out of using powerful eye contact is by justifying looking away with the claim, "I needed to look away to find the word." I challenge this claim too.

If you were talking to a dear friend in a totally unselfconscious conversation and you were intimately focused on them, would you still look away to find words as frequently as you claim is necessary? If so, fine! Your pattern is probably consistent across many communication scenarios and likely has much to do with how you choose or recall words. But often you will see that people in professional situations look away much more than they might do with a friend. In that case, the eye contact gap between those two scenarios is what we're interested in closing.

This dynamic is an important one to be aware of because when people cling to a high-frequency pattern of looking away to "find words," they risk slipping into a vicious cycle: They don't need to look away to find a word, they need to find a word because they looked away. It's a chicken-and-egg relationship. The rapid and frequent shifting of eye contact can make maintaining your stream of thought more difficult, not less! And so linguistic precision goes down the less you look at the other person. When your linguistic precision goes down, you start saying less accurate and more filler-language-riddled content. When you say less accurate and more filler-language-riddled content, you feel bad about performing poorly and therefore desire to make even less eye contact (to, in effect, hide). Thus, the vicious cycle picks up momentum.

The flip side of that pattern, of course, is a virtuous cycle, and here's a fun way to create one with an exercise that ostensibly is about eye contact but that transforms filler language. A surprising and freeing way to experiment with increasing your linguistic precision is by disciplining yourself to look consistently into the eyes of another person and choosing your words diligently as you do so. It feels strange and not particularly valuable to ramble in an unstructured monologue with tons of filler language while looking deeply into another human's eyes, so we strive to become more accurate editors and more industrious word searchers. This is a great way to reverse engineer accurate, precise content.

Let's do a hands-on activity now to explore this. On the next page, you're going to see ten squares with what look like small ink dots. In a moment, I want you to tear that page out of this book. That's right! Tear it out! Freedom yet again! Then I want you to tear along the borders of the squares so you have ten small pieces of paper and each piece has only one dot. Feel free to turn the page, rip it out, and create those ten pieces now.

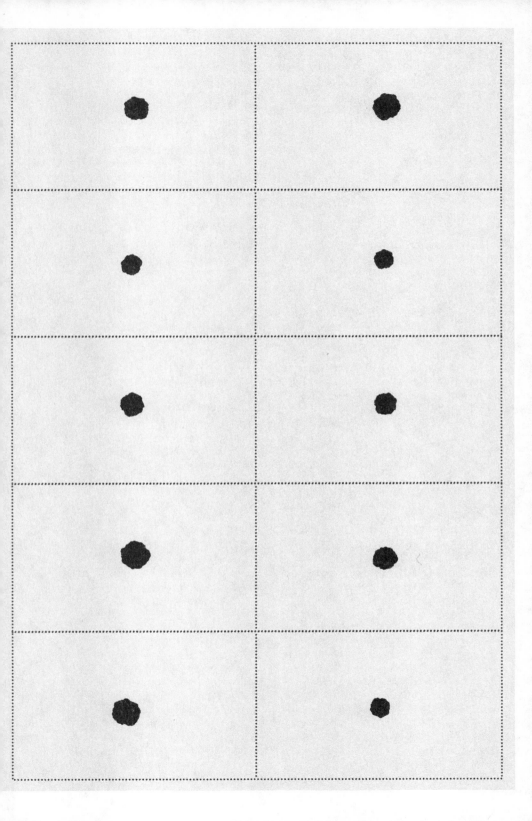

Now that you have ten mobile dots, I want you to distribute those dots in a totally random way in front of your plane of vision. Spread them out on your desk, table, furniture, floor—anywhere in front of you. Be sure you can see all of them without turning your head. If you're ambitious, scrawl dots on sticky notes so you can even place them on the walls (see the following picture).

For this experiment to work, you need to think of two roughly equivalent topics on which you can speak for about sixty seconds each. Please choose professional topics. Examples might be the following:

- Explain two specific projects you're working on.
- Tell two equal-caliber professional success stories.
- Tell two equal-caliber professional failure stories.

You can be very creative with this; the only exact criterion is that your ability to speak about these two things is roughly equal (in other words, don't choose the hilarious story you've told a thousand times about meeting your bestie and a brand-new elevator pitch). Just to make sure you're being concrete about this, please write in the titles or topics of those two areas here:

TOPIC 1: _____

_____

TOPIC 2: _____

_____

Now that you have the topics, it's time for the experiment. Without practicing or planning at all, I want you to endeavor to speak intelligently about topic 1, but to do so while shifting your eye contact among the ten dots as rapidly and randomly as possible. Shifting your eye movements chaotically around the dots dozens and dozens and dozens of times in sixty seconds is succeeding at this experiment. Go ahead and...

Do. The. Experiment. Now.

(Really. Do the exercise.)

* * *

Noooooooooow that you've done that, take away nine dots and leave only one at some easy-to-see point in front of you (not all the way down by your navel or on the ceiling). Now talk about the second topic, but this time focus on the one dot the whole time. (Please blink, of course!) Really endeavor to fix your eyes just to that one spot.

Do. That. Now.

(Really. Do the exercise.)

* * *

Thanks for participating! Your lifelong-learner credits are accumulating!

What did you notice? In exercise 1, did you feel how challenging and stressful it was to try to hold together a coherent bit of speaking while your eyes were shifting constantly and rapidly? In contrast in exercise 2, did you feel the sense of relief that came from just focusing on one? What you've just proven to yourself is how challenging you may unwittingly be making your job as a communicator. If you've developed a pattern of shifting your eyes around and rarely sustaining lengthy eye contact, you may also have developed a pattern of shifting your words and rarely sustaining a lengthy thought.

(The reason I asked you to choose two pieces of content was so you couldn't say that the added familiarity of doing the same topic twice created the improved content in exercise 2.)

As you have now hopefully come to expect, I have a kinesthetic tool for this skill too. Like the one in the last chapter, it also utilizes a ball. In the ideal version of this drill, you would have three or four partners to help. If you're solo, never fear—there is a way to do the activity (you'll just need a wall). So, please, take a moment and go get a ball or resurrect the paper ball you created last chapter.

BALL THROWING FOR EYE CONTACT

Like the ball-throwing activity for vocal fry and upward inflection you learned in Chapter 10, I'm going to ask you to warm up your throwing motion again. Why? Because this time throwing a ball is going to force you to look at your audience—specifically to see whether they are prepared and willing to catch the ball.

This is—in essence—what we do when we communicate: We throw and receive ideas. If you're observant, you may even notice how people organically gesture in some way toward their audience at the beginning and end of thoughts, "throwing" the idea to them. Imagine asking someone after a meeting if they want to go to lunch. Can you envision gently directing your hand in the other person's direction, in effect pitching (baseball) or setting (volleyball) the conversational ball to them?

Using an actual ball as a prop takes that instinctual gesture and—crucially—adds a requirement that can't be avoided: to ensure the person has the best possible chance of catching the ball, you need to look them in the eye to gauge their preparedness.

If you have a partner, this is how to do the drill. While looking at your partner consistently—without interruption—speak the first thought of your content. At the end of the thought, maintain eye contact, and assess whether the other person is ready to catch the ball. Are they looking at you? Smiling, perhaps? Focused on listening, or distracted (perhaps by their phone)? Once you have determined they are prepared to catch the ball, throw it to them! This is the only moment in the drill when you can shift your eye contact because—as every coach who ever taught a Little Leaguer knows—"you have to keep your eye on the ball." So, while the ball travels across space from your hand to your partner's, both thrower and receiver will probably focus on the ball instead of each other's eyes.

Once your listener has the ball, they get to be in control. (Whether they use that control helpfully or mischievously is up to them!) They get to choose when to throw the ball back to you. They can do so immediately; they can take their sweet time. It's up to them. As the speaker, you may not move on to the next thought in your content until you have received the ball. To know when they are going to throw it to you, you need to—you guessed it—look at them and use eye contact to gauge when the throw is coming. Once you have received the ball, you may speak the next thought in your content. If you have more than one partner in this exercise, you may now look at the second person and repeat the process for your second thought. (If you have a single partner, continue to look at and throw just to them, of course.) Practice this over and over until you ingrain the habit of holding eye contact throughout a thought for the profound and worthy purpose of seeing whether your message has been received.

If you don't have a partner to work with, you can do this drill solo. You need just two things: a wall to throw a ball against, and a bouncy ball. A racquetball, tennis ball, or foam ball works best. Then identify one roughly eye-level place on the wall to simulate the height of a human audience and focus on a real or imagined target that is about the same size as a person's face. (I sometimes have clients create a smiley face by adhering three sticky notes to the wall so they have a specific target.) Then do the exercise, maintaining eye contact with the target throughout the full length of each thought. At the end of each thought, throw the ball—accurately—at the target so that it hits it (more or less) and you're able to catch the rebound. Once you have caught the ball, put your focus back on the target and share your next thought. Proceed this way—throwing the ball at the end of each thought and breaking eye contact with that spot only for the all-important activity of catching the rebound—through each spoken thought.

SILENT STORYTELLING FOR EYE CONTACT

Remember Silent Storytelling from Chapter 9? It can be a powerful drill for eye contact. But in this version, you need some partners to work with. If you're able to gather a helper or two, try the following. Do Silent Storytelling again, but this time hold yourself to a very high standard: you need to elicit nods from each of your audience members as you "speak." Your helpers have a role to play here: They must nod if they are generally comprehending what you're saying. If not, they should gently shake their head no. If you're seeing a lot of no's, that's your cue that you're not going far enough with the activity: Your gestures, facial expressions, and enunciation aren't dynamic enough to get your ideas across without sound. If you're getting lots of nods, you're on the right track—keep it up!

What is revelatory about this application of Silent Storytelling is this: It unlocks eye contact organically, unleashing it because of the utterly human activity of striving to be understood. In the exercise, you must be looking at the other person to see whether they are understanding what you're saying or not. But—hilariously—isn't that what we should be doing all the time? Shouldn't we be striving to be understood and looking at our audience to confirm understanding? And likewise, when they are speaking to us, shouldn't we be looking at them and striving to understand them? It takes some effort to enlist helpers in this version of the exercise, but I promise it's worth it.

PRO TIP

One of the most challenging aspects of coaching speakers on eye contact is that looking directly into another human being's eyes can feel intimate. People are hesitant to experiment and practice something that can feel so intense and immediate. But it's essential that you keep a learner's mindset and explore this terrain, because eye contact is both innate and learned; your learned processes are by definition both natural and habitual. Perception and reality are infamously misaligned in this category, with people believing they have maintained eye contact most of the time when, in fact, they were rarely looking at their audience, and thinking they needed to look away to find a word when, in fact, they need to find a word because they looked away. So the coaching note is simply this: Be brave. Explore eye contact. It's worth it.

PERFORMANCE OR PRACTICE?

If ever there was a skill that was for performance, eye contact is it. The entire point of improving your eye contact is so you can accomplish the most integral task of communication: seeing whether your audience understands your message. With each of these exercises, strive to integrate them into the performance of your daily communication life.

WHAT ABOUT VIRTUAL?

Now we get to the only skill in this book that truly has different requirements for live versus virtual conversations. Gestures, posture, vocal variety, enunciation—they are all functionally the same whether you're talking to a person or to a screen. But eye contact is different, and difficulty with eye contact in video is understandable. Ordinarily, eye contact between you and your audience is a closed system—a reinforcing feedback loop in which the shared focus of two or more people reinforces a give-and-take of offering and receiving communication. The more you invest in the cycle, the more information and trust you gain.

On camera, that all breaks down. We're cast adrift in a sea of assumptions in which our ability to read our audience's intent is completely compromised. Every grimace, brow curl, or glance takes on outsized proportions. We're certain our audience is bored, intransigent, hostile, or preoccupied. And no one knows where anyone else is focusing! You can appear to be looking at someone when you're not; you can appear to be not looking at someone when you are. Shifting, wandering eyes might be searching the desktop for a relevant document, or they might be perusing social media and attending to random, unrelated notifications. Or maybe the speaker just has their video software application positioned in a weird place on their desktop? Who's to say?

It's all very mystifying.

So, this chapter's portion on virtual communication is longer than that of other chapters because there are several layers to consider.

I'm going to offer coaching explicitly to the speakers on video calls. But I ask you to consider what my suggestions imply for the listener too. Spoiler alert: The listener has to listen to and look at the speaker in an uninterrupted manner. Warning—this is hard. Video calls can be bone-numbingly boring. The World Wide Web offers no shortage of distractions. It doesn't matter. Your job—as deceptively simple as it sounds—is to pay attention to the speaker (ideally with their video box positioned in such a way on the desktop that it looks as though you're looking into the camera). I have no kinesthetic tool for you to force yourself to do that; I have no sage advice or wisdom either. It is hard. It takes mindfulness and patience and energy and mental stamina. There is nothing but to do it.

Given I have no shortcut for you the listener, let's get back to the speaker, for whom I do have some more nuanced coaching. When on video, the immediate problem to solve is this: How do you make people feel seen and heard when they don't know if you're looking at them? The answer is straightforward: you need to be looking directly at—or very near—your computer's camera.

But a second problem develops from the solution of the first: If you're staring at the camera, how do you see responses, nonverbal cues, or other indications of agreement or dissent from your audience? The answer is simple if you're on a call with just one person, but it gets more challenging the larger the audience grows.

When you are on a call with just one person, to solve both problems of eye contact: Position your listener's video tile as close to your camera as possible; then look at that person's face while you speak. If your face is a foot or so (approximately 0.3 meters) away from the screen, it will appear to your listener as if you are looking at them, and not down and away at some other spot on your screen.

You can test this with a lightning-fast activity, provided you use a computer that has a camera at the top of its screen (rather than near the keyboard). Start a video meeting in any app, record the meeting so you can watch the footage later, and then do the following: Sitting precisely as you would for a meeting, shrink the video tile of your face and position it as close to the camera at the top of the screen as possible. Now look at yourself in that video box and keep your gaze there continuously. Next, slowly move your actual face in toward the camera until your nose is almost touching the computer screen, all the while keeping your eyes focused on your video box. When you are as close to the computer as possible, shift nothing but your eyes and gaze directly into the camera lens. Now slowly move your body back to your original seated position, keeping your eyes on the camera. Then try the reverse: Move your face slowly forward toward the computer while looking directly into the camera. Once your nose is nearly touching the computer screen, shift only your eyes down to look at your video tile and then move back to your original seated position. Now stop the screen recording and watch it.

What you will discover is that when your face is about twelve inches away from the computer's camera lens, looking directly at the camera *and* looking directly at the video tile positioned just below the camera lens look pretty darn similar to your audience. When you are mere inches—or centimeters—away from the camera, the discrepancy in the appearance of eye contact is vast. But for every inch farther back you get, the distinction between gazing directly into the camera and gazing just below it decreases.

So, in video conversations with one listener, train yourself to look at their video box, which you have positioned on the screen as close to the camera lens as possible. It will read as though you are "looking directly at me."

If many people are on the call, giving the appearance of making eye contact becomes more challenging. Some software tries to solve this problem by automatically resizing and prioritizing the active speaker's video box, but sometimes it prioritizes inaccurately. It struggles when multiple people speak simultaneously. And sometimes the software positions the active speaker's tile farther away from the camera than is ideal.

If you want to make eye contact with multiple people throughout the course of the call, try the following: Keep your hand on your computer mouse and position the video tile of whomever you want to focus on near your computer's camera. The law of diminishing returns applies with this approach, though, when there are many people on the call. Don't give yourself carpal tunnel syndrome frenetically repositioning the app each and every single time a different person speaks. Play around with the approach; you'll find the right balance.

It's often simpler to choose one person and attend only to them. Remember: if you're the one speaking, everyone is watching you (theoretically); the more responsive and engaged you look with that single person, the more others on the call will feel like you're responding and engaging with them.

If you go this route, who should you choose as your primary focus? That depends on the situation, of course, but I'll give you three likely candidates. The first one is whoever is most essential on the call: a client or prospect, an interviewee or interviewer, your manager or boss, etc. The second candidate is the "best listener"—this person uses facial expressions, smiles, nods, looks into the camera, is actively engaged. The third candidate is a good one if you're up for a challenge: the person who exhibits the least responsiveness. In this case, choose the person with the fewest facial expressions, poor eye contact, and no nodding. Then challenge yourself to get this person to show some type of responsiveness. This is a higher-level-of-difficulty challenge; attempt it only in situations when you're feeling at ease or zealously inspired.

Once you've identified that person, shift the screen view so that their video box is primary, but make the entire software window small enough that you can position it close to your computer's camera. Now, through the length of the call, your job is to communicate in such a way that you elicit as many dynamic reactions from that person as possible. And look at them— the entire time—to see how involved you can keep them. This will have the side benefit of supercharging much of your delivery, and your colleagues may ask if you had an extra cup of coffee that morning. Or more likely they'll just thank you for making the call slightly less boring than their other video calls.

In an ideal world, you would be able to attend to each individual participant flawlessly while simultaneously looking directly into the camera. Tech might eventually find an elegant solution.

But for now, we're stuck with looking at a whole bunch of floating heads in boxes.

Which is... tiring. I'll leave as the subject of another book the discussion of remote communication's costs—the fatigue, challenges to our attention span, and more. Yes, looking at a screen for a long time can be exhausting. Yet it's required if you want your audience to feel that you are attending to them and care about their communication.

So build some self-care and wellness breaks into your life, but look at the camera—or very near it—if you want to demonstrate good "eye contact" on video.

While you're at it, when you're on that video call, why not get up and talk while standing. Why? You'll find out in the next chapter.

CHAPTER 13

PHYSICAL PRESENCE
PART ONE: POSTURE

How to Be as Tall as You Are

f I described someone as "being in their body," what do you think that might mean? I know it sounds like a bizarre thing to say: Where else could that person be? It's a phrase that's used widely in theater. When actors, directors, and theater professionals talk about "being in your body," what they're describing is a fully embodied performance. When actors are in their bodies, they're more responsive to their instincts, more believable as a character, and even less likely to get hurt. A heightened awareness of how your body's feeling, moving, and working in a communication situation can help you be more effective too. This is not an on/off switch, meaning, you're either in your body or not. Like many things, it's on a continuum. And the idea is that, through the course of this book, you will learn techniques to be more in your body rather than less.

Contrast that with another phrase you're probably more familiar with: *out-of-body experience*. People frequently use that phrase to characterize a moment of tremendous stage fright, nerves, or anxiety—usually around public speaking. They felt so adrenalized, so anxious, and so hyper self-focused that they didn't even feel physically present in their bodies. That's the most extreme example of being out of one's body, but we fluctuate between the two states all the time, to a greater or lesser degree. We can be more in our bodies at any given time by practicing a variety of physical and kinesthetic activities, some of which you're learning in this book.

To break this down into fundamental components, in the next three chapters we will examine physical presence in three primary areas: posture, stance, and gestures.

Speakers might struggle in each of these areas. And it's no wonder. The world conspires to make our physical lives challenging. Let's dive into posture now.

POSTURE: WHY EVERYTHING YOU THOUGHT YOU KNEW IS WRONG

As in many other communication subject areas, the coaching people get about posture often isn't helpful. And like in other chapters, my first critique is with how we name things. I've been using the word *posture* because that's how we're all accustomed to labeling our body's bearing and positioning. But going forward, I'll also refer to our posture as *use* (with an *s* sound, not a *z*, as in "I have no use for the word *posture*"). Why? Like eye contact, "posture" is all too often spoken about as though it were a possession, and a bad one at that: "I have bad posture." But posture is an activity, not an object. Posture isn't static; it's fluid, and it can be adjusted and changed and is adjusted and changed all day long as we use our bodies in better or worse and efficient or inefficient ways. So, instead of the word *posture*, I encourage you to consider substituting in the word *use* for this topic—as in, how you are using your body in any given moment.

When people are using themselves badly, the coaching typically elicited falls into thought-suppression traps, and it usually sounds like this: "Don't slouch." Not only does that instruction put your attention on a negative ("Don't think of a pink elephant"), but it also carries a subtle judgment of character—perhaps implying apathy or laziness—that goes back to scoldings you may have received from parents or teachers. It's hard not to experience that feedback as a personal criticism.

But let's say you avoid the negative ("don't slouch") and instead receive something actionable. That typically sounds like "Sit up straight" or "Pull your shoulders back." Both are actionable, but also problematic. Sitting "up straight" isn't actually how the human body achieves tall, fluid, graceful posture. To explore this, I want you to draw a line that you think represents how the human spine and its twenty-six vertebrae look from a side view. Don't pull up a picture of it on your computer or smart device; just draw from memory what you think a spine looks like. Please draw in this box:

CHAPTER 13
POSTURE

You may (I hope) have drawn something like this:

As you'll see in the visual at right, the spine is actually very curvy. It's not straight at all. So endeavoring to straighten it is not just challenging, it's impossible. And if one were to straighten it, one could do serious neurological damage. As for pulling your shoulders back (typically cranking them back in an exaggerated military stance), that adjustment usually recruits a whole series of muscles that aren't supposed to be used to keep your shoulders pinned back and your head in a vertical position. Those muscles fatigue quickly, and then the muscle exhaustion and mental discouragement of failing can boomerang and allow you to slip into even worse use.

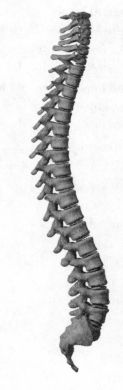

MODERN POSTURE

Why is posture so hard to get right? It's a quite discouraging reason. Western society has deeply skewed what "natural posture" is, primarily because we sit in chairs way too much. If you lived in a hunter-gatherer society in which you were walking fifteen to thirty miles a day, and chairs didn't exist, you wouldn't need to read this chapter!

In fact—assuming you are not in a hunter-gatherer society at this very moment—please observe your surroundings: If there are people around you, subtly notice their use. If you're listening to this on audio, you may well be amid a commute and able to observe a variety of strangers. What is their use like? If loved ones are near, how is their use? If you have young kids present, it's likely their use is better than yours. But even theirs, sadly, is already probably not as good as it was a few years ago.

If you're alone, you can do something different to observe your own use: freeze. Do not move your body one iota from its current position. Now, using only your arm while keeping every other part of your body still, take out your cell phone and—moving only your arm and hand— hold your phone at arm's length and take a profile photo of your head, neck, and upper torso. Then look at the photo. If you don't have a smart device handy, instead take your finger, draw it slowly along the side perimeter of your body, and ask yourself what letter shape your finger just traced (likely, it's something like a C).

Undoubtedly, the various bodies you just observed—including your own—look less than ideal in terms of their use. Do you have chronic neck or back pain? If you do, you're in good company. Roughly a third of American adults report something similar. If you're living in any other highly industrialized nation, there's a good chance your statistics are similar. Chairs profoundly corrupt what is natural use. Computers, cell phones, air, car, and train travel—all these things make matters worse. It's not an exaggeration to say that modern society is designed to screw up your use. Which is why the first thing people tell me when I provide coaching on their posture is: "This doesn't feel natural." I always ask them next, "What does feel natural?" Inevitably, they contort their body into some torturous position that drops their height by three inches or more, puts all their weight on one leg, erases any space in their lower back, and collapses the length of their cervical spine.

The sad news is we don't know what natural posture is anymore. If we spent more time standing and moving, we would not have such a deeply compromised sense of natural posture. We would be even better if we added squatting to that equation too.

What is squatting? It is the position you assume when you allow your knees to bend as deeply as they can while keeping your weight evenly dis- tributed on both feet, which are planted roughly hip distance apart.

The human body is designed to do this quite comfortably—for long spans of time. If you've ever seen pictures of folks in indigenous societ- ies working in a squatting position—trading goods or having a meal— you might recognize the position. You used to be able to do this, by the way. Kids do it all the time, totally organically. Look at this picture of my son when he was a toddler and his flawless squatting form. Or check out my daughter, squatting on the back of the couch, perched on the furniture like a canary. As a parent, I have tried to teach my kids many skills. Squatting wasn't one of them. It's not a thing we learn; we just do.

And then we lose the ability to do! Likely, you can't squat as well as my kids in these photos, or as well as you could when you were their age. If you don't believe me, check right now. If you're in a place where you can stand and test this, please do. Get up … and then squat.

Seriously. Bring this book with you, get into a squat, and keep reading. To get into this position—if you can—you'll probably need to position your feet a little wider than hip distance apart with your toes pointing out slightly. Young kids can easily do a squat with their hips, knees, and feet all in line. You (provided you're not a five-year-old savant reading this book that features fancy, erudite words like *savant*) probably can't.

If this squat creates any pain whatsoever, don't do it!! Safety first, people. If you have a knee or hip injury, it may be that you can't reclaim your squat without doing a physical therapy or exercise regimen. And this book can't substitute for either of those. But if you're able to try this safely, please do.

So make whatever adjustments you need to experience squatting. If it's unreasonably difficult, you can try two alternatives to make it easier.

One, if you have very comfortable high-heeled shoes, you can wear them while you squat. (Heels make squatting easier for most people because they compensate for tight Achilles tendons.) If you don't have comfy heels, just squat on a slightly inclined plane. Any kind of uneven surface will do: the side of a hill, a ramp, and so forth. And if you need an even simpler solution, put a rolled-up towel or something similar under your heels so that they're slightly higher than your toes.

If you haven't already, please try some version of a squat now.

First, are you able to accomplish the position? Can you squat? Probably...but with some balance issues and massive muscular effort. Do you feel a tremendous amount of strain in your Achilles tendons? Or are you using an exhausting amount of muscle effort in the front of your calves to keep yourself from falling backward?

This difficulty is because your muscles and skeleton do not work as flexibly and fully as they would if you had spent the last years and decades standing, moving, and squatting.

If you're still in the squat (you may have fallen or given up!), you're likely already getting tired. This used to be easy.

If you want to improve your posture (use), a worthy mission is to reclaim your ability to squat. So intervention number one to improve your use is to squat for a few minutes every day. While you're doing it, I want you to go through the following subtle physical adjustments and visualizations using this checklist:

- Visualize your tailbone dropping lower and even descending into the floor.
- Allow your neck to be free and long as you keep your eyes focused on the horizon, not collapsed into the floor or craning up toward the ceiling.
- Breathe into your lower back and escape the typical shallow chest breathing that plagues our day-to-day.
- To the extent you're able, release the muscular effort (probably most acutely felt in the front of your calves) you're using to stay in this position and focus more on balance than effort. To help, focus on releasing the tension in your butt,

thighs, and the front of your calves, and instead cultivate a heavy, wide, grounded feeling in your feet.

Why is squatting so good? Well, if you did that exercise, you probably already felt why! Among other things, it allows the spine to be as long as it actually is; it reclaims room in the lower back into which the lungs can fully expand; and it gives a natural stretch to the hips, which for most adults in modern society are chronically—even cripplingly—tight.

This was—and can be again—a "natural" posture. But the fact that it now feels so unnatural is an indication of how far from natural we have shifted.

Therefore, giving people the suggestion to "just be natural" may not help whatsoever if their "natural" has become this:

NATURAL POSTURE

Let's talk for a second about what good, natural posture—or use—is. As we saw previously, the spine is a wave—a series of counterbalanced curves that allow for free, elongated movement. So a much better mantra to give yourself rather than "Stand up straight" is simply this statement: "Be as tall as you actually are." Most people who are five foot nine are walking around life being five foot seven. Ditto for those five foot two, three foot eleven, seven foot one, and six foot five. If you prefer the metric system, the same is true for your height in centimeters.

So, how do you achieve your full height? Well, I'm going to walk you through a couple of visualization exercises and then some physical adjustments to help you experience what it feels like to be as tall as you are. Height isn't everything, but focusing on it is a quick way to get closer to what "good" use looks like without falling into the counterproductive "stand up straight" and "pull your shoulders back" adjustments.

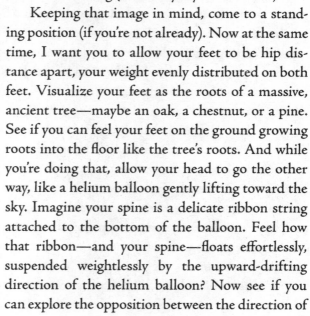

To achieve your actual height, I want you to begin by imagining that your head is a helium balloon, floating gently toward the ceiling (or the sky if you're outside).

Keeping that image in mind, come to a standing position (if you're not already). Now at the same time, I want you to allow your feet to be hip distance apart, your weight evenly distributed on both feet. Visualize your feet as the roots of a massive, ancient tree—maybe an oak, a chestnut, or a pine. See if you can feel your feet on the ground growing roots into the floor like the tree's roots. And while you're doing that, allow your head to go the other way, like a helium balloon gently lifting toward the sky. Imagine your spine is a delicate ribbon string attached to the bottom of the balloon. Feel how that ribbon—and your spine—floats effortlessly, suspended weightlessly by the upward-drifting direction of the helium balloon? Now see if you can explore the opposition between the direction of your head and the direction of your feet. Continue to allow your head to float away and your feet to grow roots. Now, pause. You probably have just added an inch or two to your height. That is what good natural posture, or use, looks like. Notice, hopefully, that you're not using an extraordinary amount of muscle effort to keep your body in this position.

If you have a background in yoga, martial arts, tai chi, the Alexander Technique, meditation, or the performing arts, such as acting, dancing, singing, or playing music, you may already have positive postural muscle memory you can resurrect. The exercises you will learn in this chapter—like the helium balloon one—unlock some of the same improvements as those other disciplines, approaches, and methods. If you are familiar with any of them, I encourage you to bring their focus on posture into your professional life.

Actors and performers use those tools, but they also "gamify" studying posture. One interesting theater game of this sort explores status and how humans consciously and unconsciously respond to it.

Sit back and imagine you're in year one of acting conservatory. Sort of like playing a silly poker game, this drill requires people to wear labels on their body that can only be seen by others around them, but not by themselves. The game goes by various names and is played with two sets of characters: one monarch and their subjects. One person gets a card or sign indicating Monarch. Everyone else gets one labeled Subject. No one can see their own card (typically worn on the back or forehead). All are instructed to walk around the room and interact. Players are not allowed to reveal to one another what is written on the cards, but they are instructed to show through their behavior who is the monarch and who are subjects. They may not ruin the game by referring to the monarch by *liege* or *majesty* or *sire* or *king* or *queen*, but they can do anything else physically and vocally to indicate who is the most powerful person in the room. You play the game until the monarch deciphers their identity.

In terms of posture, what happens? The monarch gets taller and taller as the game goes on, carrying themselves more regally as ever more people genuflect to them.

You likely don't have a bunch of acting-school classmates at the ready, willing to play a rousing round of this game. But you have the next best thing—a crown! On the next page you will find a paper crown that can be cut out in four strips, shaped into a ring roughly the circumference of your head, taped, and worn. You, too, can be Communication Monarch for a day.

When you're ready, I want you to embrace your arts and crafts skills again and put together the crown on the following page. Once you've done that, come back to this text. I will await your bidding, my liege....

* * *

Now that you have a paper crown that substantiates your claims of sovereignty, you get to stand like it! In a moment I want you to place the crown on your head, stand like the regal figure you are, and deliver some content. Ready, proclaim away!

* * *

What happened? Were you able to be as tall as you actually are? Did the ground under your feet shake with the royal weight of your proclamations? If not, adjust your crown, and try it again—this time with an even more regal bearing.

Please notice how you stand in this exercise. If your head and neck are more elevated and elongated, with more graceful use than normal, why not try playing Monarch for an hour some time? Then maybe even Monarch for a day. I'll leave the decision to wear the crown or not to you (some of you might be able to get away with it), but regardless of whether you're wearing it, act like you're wearing it.

I know and trust that you will save that crown, that it will become a coveted talisman across many societies, and that eventually—in the ages to come when people sing new songs of your old glories—it will become a relic. But in case you lose this crown, or it gets eaten by the dog, here's a simple way to achieve the same result. Practice standing while keeping a book or a flat object balanced on the top of your head. To keep the book level, the body tends to use its full height to maintain that balance. Of course, you can't stand with a book on your head in many places, but it's a good thing to practice from time to time by yourself, and it comes in handy if you can't find your crown.

For that exercise, simply find a pad of paper or lightweight book. I would say you could use this one if you're reading it in hard copy, but then you couldn't read the rest of this chapter! So find a different book or a pad

CHAPTER 13 POSTURE

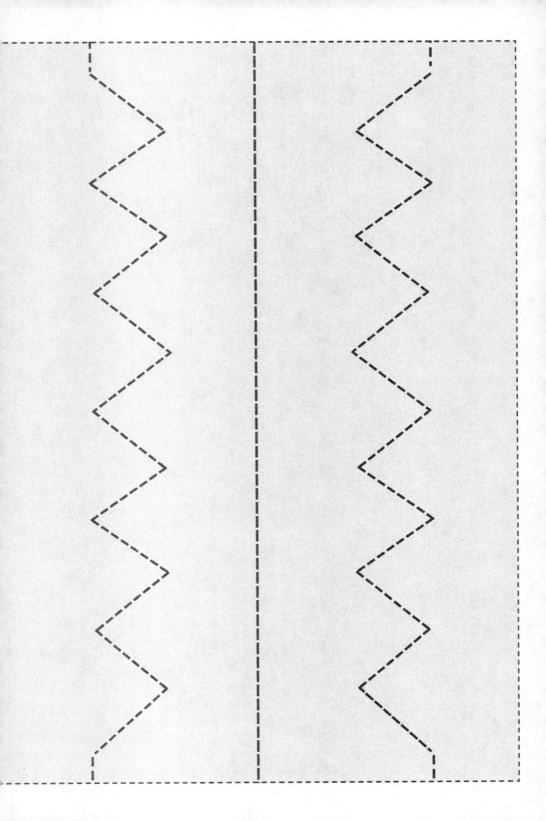

of paper. The prop must be rigid enough that it can remain flat on top of your head (hardcover books work best). Once you have the prop, use the visualization and postural adjustment flow we just went through to find your own tall, released, long posture. Then place the book or pad on your head. When you think you have it balanced, move your hand away. Then practice speaking some content. Your job is to see how long you can speak while keeping the prop on your head.

Take a moment to get a prop and let's do it now!

*   *   *

How long were you able to do it? Note the time, and try it again, but this time strive for longer.

You may have had an uncontrollable desire to walk while doing that exercise, as you couldn't help but test keeping the object in place while moving. In fact, if you haven't yet, try moving now. It increases the challenge even more. It's also a good preview for the next chapter when we get into movement. But fight the urge to jump ahead. We still have some ground to cover on posture, like...how to sit.

SITTING

You might be saying, "This is all well and good, but what about the position we all find ourselves in many hours a day—sitting?" I've already mentioned that the more you can get out of your chair and move around the better. So, the first note would be to get up!

But when you have no choice but to sit, you can still do it with better use. If you're not sitting already (in which case, I applaud you!), please do. Now as well as you're able, sit on the palms of your hands, with your palms up. What you'll feel is the bony protuberances of your pelvis. Yoga teachers and other movement professionals often colloquially call these your "sits bones." Take a moment and rock around a bit. Feel those strong, stable points? The image I want you to bring to mind is this: Those bones are the feet of your torso. Just as when you are in an ideal standing position, your feet are the strong, rooted foundation of your posture, and the bottom of your pelvic girdle is your torso's feet. Next, gently and slowly pull your hands out from under you, but please try to experience the sensation of those bones sinking into the chair just as heavily as your feet anchored into the floor in the tree-root visualization exercise. Allow your "torso feet" to support your whole upper body. Now focus on the other polarity: Same as in the standing version, please visualize your head as a helium balloon lifting ever so gently off the long string of your spine. Take a moment or two to enjoy the height you have just attained.

All the exercises you've just learned are intended to help you experience what good use actually looks and feels like, both seated and standing. But finding good is the easy part. Here's the hard part: Now that you have found good, how do you keep it? Your job is not to maintain this constantly but to allow yourself to regain this physical bearing when you inevitably notice you've lost it (that is, you're slouching).

I suggest finding ways to remind yourself that don't involve thinking or remembering. Consider: If thinking about having good posture and trying to remember to "stand up straight" were the answers, wouldn't you have already attained flawless posture?

So, I suggest you outsource the remembering and thinking. You don't need to remember or think; you need to do. Here are some options.

- First, evaluate the chairs you regularly use when you work, eat, and watch. My suggestions fit in two categories: (1) eliminate (that is, spend less time sitting); and (2) optimize (use better chairs when you do).
- *Eliminate*: Whenever possible, see if you can substitute a standing position for a seated one. Consider getting a standing workstation. Don't let cost or procrastination slow you; if you don't want to buy one, make one. In college one of my friends was baffled to see me typing an essay for class with my computer on top of my dresser and the keyboard placed on the opened second drawer. I won't tell you how many years ago that was, but suffice it to say that I wasn't using a wireless keyboard. I suppose that timeline makes me a trailblazer for adopting standing workstations, albeit this one was in my dorm-room closet. So, if you don't have a standing workstation, create one!

Use cardboard boxes, stacks of books, whatever you have. Then the goal is not to never sit again. You should strive simply to stand for more time than you currently are and go back and forth from seated to standing positions every so often. The goal in both positions is the same—have the best use that you can, more of the time.

* *Optimize:* Consider getting better chairs. I won't dive into the nitty-gritty of the almost limitless numbers and types of chairs out there but rather will give you a basic direction: All you're looking for is a chair that fosters the seated position we explored earlier. Try a few, do the exercises we explored in this chapter, and see which chairs enable that most readily. Or if you feel audacious, consider forgoing the chair altogether and getting a large yoga ball as a substitute! Then just sit on that. If colleagues, friends, and neighbors give you odd looks, tell them you're working on your spinal health and improving your communication, and give them a copy of this book.

◆ Position actual and/or perceptible reminders in your physical space.

* Sticky notes work well for the actual reminders: Write some encouraging postural message on them and then put them everywhere. That message could be a word, a mantra, a doodle, a stick figure, a shape—whatever is meaningful to you. If you choose words, please choose words that remind you that posture is an activity of undoing, of releasing, of freeing. It is not an activity of muscle tension. An obvious choice would be *Use.* If you want other suggestions, consider writing something (1) instructional, like "be as tall as I am," "be fully 170 cm," or "float my head"; (2) liberating, like "free," "release," or "length"; or (3) visual, like "balloon," "tree," or "sky." If you want to use a drawing, I invite you to unleash your inner artist and draw a representative or expressionist image—maybe a balloon, tree, or swan. In the posture lesson of my Executive Presence course in GK

Training's online learning programs, I suggest that viewers go a step further and modify not just their physical space but also their physical wardrobe: I ask them to staple some piece of paper into their upper garment tag to give them an unmistakable mnemonic that is literally on their skin. These are just suggestions. You can modify your physical space in countless ways, so search for what works for you.

* What are some *imperceptible* reminders?

   ○ You can use a mirror. Throughout your day, note the mirrors you see in the bathroom, hallway, entryway, work lobby, and other places. (The only ones that aren't applicable are the rear and sideview mirrors in cars.) With each mirror you encounter throughout the day, try this imperceptible reminder system. The next time you look into a mirror, note what is behind you. Specifically, look for what is obscured by your head, and therefore what appears in the mirror at the same height as the crown of your head. For example, in a bathroom mirror it might be a specific shelf that is at the same height as the reflection of your head. Then do the various postural adjustments you've learned in this chapter and see if you can make the object you've noted "go lower." What you're doing, of course, is making yourself taller so that the reference object loses altitude in the perspective of the mirror. Then choose whatever new object is now level with your head. Whenever you see yourself in that mirror, your job is to ensure that your head is at the same height as the higher object.

   ○ That technique has an easy and obvious corollary in remote video communication, which is the second imperceptible reminder to practice that I'll mention. When you're on video calls, do the same thing, but utilize something in your video call background (assuming you're not using a virtual one).

○ Here's a third: use your smartphone as a trigger to embrace better use. For a week, try reading any text on your phone or tablet by holding it up to your face rather than contorting your face, neck, and head down to the screen. If it helps, put a sticky note on the back of the phone or adjust the screensaver or wallpaper of your phone to remind you each time you pick it up.

PRO TIP

The primary way that people mess themselves up when focusing on posture is using too much muscular effort. As I outlined earlier in the chapter, upright vertical posture need not be a heavy lift. As you start this journey, it is safe to assume you'll use excessive muscular exertion in your lower back, between your shoulder blades, and in the back of your neck. Expect it because it's probably going to happen. Each time you feel yourself doing that, the correct adjustment is not to work even harder with more muscular tension, nor is it to collapse and give up and let your skeleton surrender entirely to gravity. Rather, use the tools of this chapter with relaxation and ease. Float your head to the ceiling; be as tall as you are; allow your body to release into length. It takes practice, but it's worth it.

PRACTICE OR PERFORMANCE?

The drills in this chapter vary widely between practice and performance. For example, each of the ways to make a postural focus imperceptible—striving to meet an ambitious height line in the mirror or on video or reading information on your smartphone with your arm held high—are obviously performance drills; that is, they can be done with full expression in front of any audience. The book-on-the-head tool is obviously practice only. Visualizing your head as a balloon and your feet like tree trunks or walking through your day imagining you are a monarch are interventions that are perfectly appropriate for performance, though you can also practice on your own at any time. (I might suggest you don't actually don a paper crown unless your primary public speaking venue is teaching elementary school.)

WHAT ABOUT VIRTUAL?

Virtual communication is fraught terrain for posture. Yet within that fraught terrain lies tremendous potential. If you happen to be reading this on a desktop computer, you know exactly what I mean because there is a good chance you're slumped in a chair, possibly propping up the bowling ball that is your head on your palm or fist.

Even if you're not looking at these words on a desktop screen, do an activity right now: Take on the shape of how you normally sit when you're in virtual meetings. Be honest with yourself! Don't be the person who lies to themselves at the dentist about how much they floss! Just take on that posture now.

There is a good reason you're likely slumping. Much of our remote communication forces us to spend hours staring straight forward at a small(ish) screen. There are architectural adjustments that can be made of course—some of which I have encouraged you to embrace in this chapter and book, such as sitting on a yoga ball or creating or procuring a standing workstation. But even with all that, the probability is high that some non-insignificant portion of your work hours is spent looking at a screen in a position that makes it challenging to maintain good posture.

It's worth grappling with that challenge, though, because remote communications offer an ideal practice ground. So write those sticky notes, get those yoga balls, identify that ambitious background height marker, and make posture a consistent focus when you're remote.

Wherever you practice and focus on posture, though, be kind to yourself as you explore. Like our breath, how we stand and move are central parts of our journey through the world. Just like improving your habits around diet, exercise, or sleep, any incremental improvement is better than none. So if you can allow better use five minutes per day, that's better than three, and seven is better than five, and eleven is better than seven, and sixteen is better than eleven. Start anywhere. But start. Your breath, brain, and body will all thank you.

Speaking of your body, posture is just one part of physical presence. It's time we move on to the others. Stance and movement are next.

CHAPTER 14

PHYSICAL PRESENCE PART TWO: STANCE AND MOVEMENT

How to Stand Still (or Not)

L et's start by appreciating your feet.

Your feet are unsung heroes in your life. Most of the time we just complain about them—from their aesthetics to their maintenance to the pain certain shoes elicit in them. But consider the hard work they do each day and the astonishing mechanical elegance that allows them to absorb shock, maintain balance, create stability, and enable movement.

I'm guessing you haven't thought about your feet at any point today unless they hurt. We take them for granted, but we shouldn't. They allow us to be upright!

Before you think I'm being overly complimentary of basic functioning, remember: Standing has to be learned. We work very hard as individuals to gain that skill. If you've ever witnessed a baby learning to stand (by falling countless times), you know what I'm talking about.

And we worked very hard as a species to attain the ability to stand. Bring to mind the posture of chimpanzees, gorillas, orangutans, baboons, and any other primate save humans for an instant visual contrast.

It is a hard-won skill, both as individuals and as a species. In this chapter, we'll give it the appreciation it's due, both because it's miraculous and because we must first master the primary task of standing before we can advance to moving.

Is it okay just to "stand there"? My briefest answer: yes. If I'm coaching someone on stance, one theme that often comes up is their discomfort with staying stationary, usually encapsulated by the inquiry, "Does it look weird if I just stand here?" My response? "Let's film so you can see for yourself." I set up their phone with their entire body in the camera frame. Then I have them present some material two times. The first time they are required to stand in one position with grounded feet. They have full permission to gesture with complete abandon, but they are not permitted to move their feet. The second time they are allowed to "do what's natural."

Next, I do something duplicitous: I pretend to turn off their camera, but I continue recording. I ask them about their experience of the exercise, and I also tell them a personal story. I do both of those things because I want to get their focus entirely off their performance. To do that, I give them a chance to talk candidly and spontaneously about their own experience and listen to a story about someone else's experience (mine).

Then and only then do I press Stop on the video recording. I reveal my dishonesty. We have a laugh about it and then get to the important work of evaluating the footage we just created.

Here's what is fascinating: Inevitably, clips 1 and 3 look similar. Clip 2 is the outlier. In it, they appear shifty, uncomfortable, uncertain where to stand, how to move, even how "to be." The takeaway is as simple as it is revelatory: Humans were designed to stand upright, and when we're not in a vicious cycle of self-focus, we tend to do as we're designed. I don't suggest that people maintain tall posture with grounded, stationary feet because they need to "exude presence," "own their power," or "stand and deliver." I suggest it because that's what humans do when they're focused on the true purpose of communication: reaching the other person.

Why do those poor forlorn souls I coach misperceive their positioning so profoundly? Why do they think they are standing effectively when in fact they're shifting constantly or wobbling precariously or rocking incessantly? As we've explored before, their perception doesn't match reality. They think they're doing one thing when actually it's another. What do they think they're doing? Being "natural."

To them, being natural has come to mean an elaborate concoction of movements and poses that imply ease, casualness, or idiosyncrasy but that untether them from efficiency in communication. This pattern looks different in different people, but I'll describe a few of the most frequent manifestations I see. You might relate to one of these.

There are: (1) the rockers, those who move their full weight back and forth, often rhythmically front to back, side to side, or sometimes even in a fully realized pattern of pacing; (2) the shifters, relatives of the rockers, who transition their full weight from one leg to another, resting in between each shift so that they essentially never weight both feet at the same time; and (3) the contortionists, those who believe their natural position features one leg constricted around the other, perhaps standing with one foot in front of the other or with the left foot shifted over in front of the right or vice versa so that their feet are actually in reverse position.

If it sounds like I'm describing a curious subset of tribes from a long-lost civilization, this is not to ridicule these patterns or these people! Trust me, however odd my descriptions sound, they're nothing compared to how odd these people assess their own performances to be when they watch their video. They feel as though they're observing someone unrecognizable, a person who moves in alien ways that make no sense and have no relationship to their subject matter.

Why is it so hard for them to simply stand? One of the first barriers to overcome is that they need to accept what I call "the stasis of standing." Standing like I've described requires being stationary, fully at rest. You are ready to move if needed, but only if needed. If it is not needed, stillness is sufficient. If you are someone who struggles with tolerating silence in a conversation, you probably intuit the anxiety this creates for some.

This is not to say that standing is not active—it is. It requires subtle adjustments and readjustments to stay upright comfortably. When standing, you likely move occasionally to relieve muscle fatigue or unweight a joint, but the frequency never approaches the rapid-fire movement that often plagues presenters who haven't built comfort with standing.

A story might be instructive. I once coached a former American football player whose position was cornerback. If you're not familiar with American football, a cornerback is tasked with preventing an opposing team's player from catching the ball. They must run in lockstep with the opposing player to be near enough to deflect or intercept the ball—all without fouling the opposing player. It is a position often played by the best athletes on the roster.

I give all this background to make a point: This person was not unskilled at using his feet, both to stand and to move. Yet when he showed me his public speaking habits, I was looking at a person who was so lopsided he could be pushed over by a light wind.

I made this point with the following exercise. I asked him to guard me as though I were one of his former opponents. I told him I was going to try to run to a point on the opposite side of the room, where a mythical quarterback would deliver me a perfectly timed pass. Instinctively and instantly, he leaped to a balanced, alert, and powerful stance. I bolted for the light switch on the far right of the room. Even in dress shoes, his athleticism was absurd. My route was vanquished within steps.

Then I showed him a still frame of video from one of his presentations and asked him to assume that pose. He was forced to take on a torturously complex leg twist, in which his feet were crisscrossed and one knee was buckled back, almost to hyperextension.

I reached the light switch easily.

What does this prove, besides the fact that it's lucky I pursued a career in communications instead of professional football? This person had cast aside an entire lifetime of top-notch muscle memory in one physical discipline (football) for a received idea of what "natural" should look like in another physical discipline (speaking). Once we connected playing cornerback to talking, his stance went from a weakness to a strength, as did his communication. What he was trying to do was in fact the very definition of unnatural, and all he had to do was remind himself of what he already knew how to do: stand with stillness, ready to move if needed.

If you're in a location that allows you to come to a standing position, please do. Please keep in mind that most locations would qualify. If you're alone in a private space, you have no excuse not to do this! If you're in an office with others, stand up and continue reading. Passersby or colleagues will only see a person momentarily escaping the death traps that are chairs. If you're riding on rapid transit and have a secure way to stand, be a Good Samaritan and give up your seat to a fellow passenger. If you're not in one of those locations, please dog-ear this page and come back to it when you are able to stand.

First, just stand. Your hands can move if needed; your face can move, your breath, your diaphragm. But your feet must remain still.

Now we'll start by reinvigorating the posture (use!) visualization from last chapter and then go further. Center your feet under you, roughly hip distance apart, feeling the ground or floor firmly beneath you. Rock forward slightly on the balls of your feet and back onto your heels. Do that a time or two until you feel absolutely balanced in the center. Now visualize your feet as the roots of a tree growing into the earth or as mounds of clay baking solid in the sun or as globs of cookie dough just in the oven slowly cooking and settling, their edges expanding ever so slightly with the weight of their congealing butter and brown sugar.

Once your feet feel wedded to the ground, focus on your calves and Achilles. Release all the tension in them. Invite your Achilles tendons to relax and feel your lower legs—especially the back of your lower legs—descending to the floor.

Move next to your knees. What miraculous joints they are! If you think you have a "bum" knee or a "bad" knee, I will posit that the opposite is true. You have a great knee—one that has somehow navigated through all manner of injury, inflammation, arthritis, and whatnot to still grudgingly or graciously do its hinging activity many, many times each day. Give some gratitude to your knees and then allow them to have a tiny bend. Remember: Standing is active. I don't mean that you should be in a deep knee bend (or even a gentle plié, to use a ballet term) but that your knees should be centered and active, keeping you vertical through efficient alignment that allows balance and symmetry to defy gravity and keep you upright.

Now move to your pelvis; visualize it as a round bowl, feeling as though it were a globe upon which the rest of your torso floats. At the same time, release tension in three places: release your butt, release your gut, and release your jaw. We often hold tension in our butt and hips—let that go. We frequently suck in our tummies—let that go. We typically clench our jaws—let that go. Once more: release your butt...your gut...your jaw.

Next, bring your attention to your shoulders. Let them melt down the trunk of your body, as though your trapezius muscles (those are the inevitably tight muscles between the base of your neck and your shoulders—where the straps of a backpack might sit) were sticks of butter slowly melting on a warm summer sidewalk. As they melt, imagine you are carrying small bags of sand in your hands, and the weight of that sand is gently pulling your hands, forearms, upper arms, and shoulders down. Don't allow this to pull you forward into a slouch or a slump; your spine is a long ribbon attached to the helium balloon of your head. The arms and shoulders release down and away, but that release doesn't roll you forward—it reinforces the balance and alignment you're already finding.

Next feel the top of your chest (where your clavicle—or collarbone—stretches across the front of your body) and back (as if you drew a line between the tops of your scapulae, or shoulder blades) expand and connect. With each rise and fall of your breath, feel the loop that circumscribes your body at that point getting larger and more released, like a gradual opening of the aperture of a camera lens.

Finally, come back to your head. Just as you learned to do last chapter, visualize it as a helium balloon lifting gently off that long ribbon string of your spine.

Those of you who may happen to be reading this book while on rapid transit have both an impediment and an advantage over the rest. Quick story: When I was in acting conservatory at NYU, the other students and I would play a game when riding the NYC subway. Provided there was enough room in a given car (rush hour was not an ideal time to play), we would stand in the middle of the subway car and let go of our grasp of any stabilizing handholds, bars, or straps. Then we would try to stay as balanced as possible, focusing solely on our stance and use, even while the car rocked and shimmied and jerked randomly. We didn't stand like surfers or snowboarders, feet several feet apart and arms aloft to counterbalance in case of falling. No, we tried to stand upright, like proud members of a wedding party. Inevitably, a significant enough jolt would come along to force us to move our feet. But even while moving we strived to keep our spines long and released, our heads aloft, our feet balanced under us supporting our weight.

If a visual of angsty acting students—who can't stop thinking about their craft long enough to read a dang book on the subway!—comes to mind, you might not be too far off. But now you get to be the angsty acting student. If you are traveling on rapid transit of some kind and can safely stand, do so. *But don't let go of the handhold!* You can get all the benefit of this exercise with none of the risk, so keep holding on to something to brace yourself. Now go through the entire progression you just learned, from the soles of your feet to the tip of your head, and see how balanced you can remain even while the transport beneath you moves of its own accord.

If you want a fun image that distills this entire progression into a single visual, imagine that you are a broomstick, your head is the broom, your body the stick, and your feet the fingertip of some giant invisible street performer who can balance an inverted broomstick on one finger even while riding a unicycle and juggling with the other hand. Keep that broom head aloft and balanced with elegance and ease, not effort.

For those of you not on rapid transit, fear not—I have not wasted three paragraphs of your life. Wherever you are, do this exercise too. Imagine you are on some type of transit; imagine the train car or bus or sci-fi hovercraft shifts and changes unpredictably; keep your stance grounded, your spine long, your use relaxed even through those shakes and shimmies. Try that for a moment.

*   *   *

CHAPTER 14
STANCE AND MOVEMENT

Take inventory of how you feel. Depending on how thoroughly you just did that progression, you are likely standing and demonstrating better use. Enjoy it. Note where physical discomfort and fatigue have lessened. Consider how many centimeters of height you have gained. Recognize how much deeper and easier your breath is. This is what good use feels like, and I want you to memorize that feeling so you can find it again when you revert to habit.

You may be eager to move on to moving, but we can't move until we've explored stillness sufficiently—and we're not quite there yet. Now that you have explored standing silently, we have to add speaking, because the phrase isn't "Stand"; it's "Stand and Deliver," so we have to get to the delivering.

You just learned how to stand well. Next, we'll ensure you're stationary. And then we'll practice talking while being stationary.

To ensure you are in fact being stationary, you get to make some choices. Each of these drills is fun, so try them all! But they all teach the same thing, so please know that if you're only able to do one or two, the takeaway is the same.

DRILL 1: PAGE STANDING

The first drill is the best one if you have a physical copy of this book. Speaking of this book, I hope it is building a foundation upon which you can stand and see a whole new frontier of communication possibilities for yourself. So why not stand on it literally?

Don't turn yet, but after you turn the page, you are going to see the silhouette of two footprints. In a moment I'm going to ask you to put the book on the floor and stand with your feet positioned on those silhouettes, holding open the pages. It is your job to keep those pages pressed to the floor (and—not coincidentally—your feet pressed to the floor as well).

If possible, I want you to take your shoes off and do this exercise barefoot or wearing socks. Why? Because—as an extra-credit activity—I'm going to ask you to turn a page, and that's monumentally difficult with shoes on.

This is how the drill goes. Choose some speaking content. Stand on the book, where indicated. Start talking. Keep the pages adhered securely to the ground. Don't let the pages lift off the floor at all. Continue to speak, allowing the task of keeping the pages down to enforce stillness in your feet. Once you have the hang of that and have been speaking for a few minutes with stationary feet, add a layer of difficulty. Every few minutes, try to turn a page with your foot. It doesn't matter whether you turn one page or many—we're practicing stance, not counting—so don't be hard on yourself. As soon as you have turned the page, stand on the pages again, adhere them to the ground, and continue talking. Do that as many times as you like to get the full benefit of the drill.

If you break the binding of this book from standing on it…good! You—and your feet—will have better understanding and skill with stance, and the sacrifice of this book's spine will have been well worth it.

DRILL 2: FLOUR STANDING

This next drill is messy, but if you're able to do it, you will never forget it. You need three things: (1) common baking flour; (2) a floor you can easily clean, upon which you can dash handfuls of flour; and (3) the willingness to clean up handfuls of flour.

You probably already have a sense of how the drill works just by hearing the ingredient list. You guessed it—your job is to take a couple handfuls of flour, get into a stable, stationary position, dash the handfuls of flour on and around your feet, and then practice speaking without disturbing the flour around the edges of your feet. This drill is especially good for those who have a stubborn perception–reality gap, because the evidence of your movement or lack thereof is unmissable in the flour.

If you ever made snow angels as a kid and remember the experience of trying to get up and out of the impression your body made in the snow without disturbing the outline of the angel, the mechanism of this drill will be familiar.

After the drill, clean up the flour (just sayin').

DRILL 3: BALL THROWING FOR STANCE

This next drill is a powerful way to focus on both stance and gestures because it requires your feet to be stationary and your arms and hands to be fluid and mobile. Therefore, we'll revisit it in the gestures chapter coming up, but with a slightly different focus. It requires a ball that has a degree of bounce. Tennis or racquetballs work best, but Wiffle balls and small rubber balls will also do the trick.

First, please find a ball. Next, position yourself standing near enough to any wall that you can easily throw the ball against it (underhand or overhand) and catch the rebound.

To start, just warm up your coordination by throwing the ball against the wall and catching it. Once you've got that cooking, I want you to add speaking. Please use professional content. As you speak, you must do two contradictory activities: (1) you must keep your feet stationary while you (2) throw the ball to as many extreme locations on the wall as you can—while still being able to catch the rebound. Your arms and hands should have to move all around the largest possible range of motion that your wingspan can handle. Keep the feet anchored to the floor. You may not move them. You may not even stand on your tiptoes to catch a high throw. For this drill, your feet are in heavy, wet beach sand, or even concrete. Throw the ball off the wall high, low, right, left—everywhere. Extra credit if some of the catches get far enough out from the central axis of your body that you must lean slightly or even bend your knees to catch. Also make sure you throw and catch some with each hand. Don't just cater to your dominant one.

Throughout this whole exercise, continue to speak your content. It may take some time to get the coordination down, and your content might not be stellar as a significant amount of your mindshare is dedicated to just catching the ball. I don't care about your content in this context though. What do I care about? The fact that your feet are entirely stationary and that you have learned how to attain stillness with them.

Now that you have attained that stillness, we can finally move....

MOVEMENT

First, do you even need to move when speaking? You just learned how to stand with stillness and talk. Perhaps that's good enough? For some communication situations, it certainly is. If you are giving a commencement address at an institution of higher learning and you're delivering remarks from behind a podium, not only should you not walk around the stage but also if you did, you would likely lose track of your content. In that scenario stillness and stance are the primary skills. But if you are in a situation in which movement is possible, should you?

Yes. Try it! Why? Just like vocal variety, physical variety is one way to offer your audience novelty: You are literally changing locations. They get to see and hear a message delivered from different positions. That's an example of movement just to change up the picture your audience sees. There are more sophisticated reasons too, like the practice of anchoring that professors use to embed content in different locations in their lecture halls that I already described (Chapter 5, for those who like to read back).

Those are some answers to the question, Why move? But to make this fundamental, let me ask a more provocative question: Why not? So long as the movement is intentional, why wouldn't you find some opportunity to take advantage of a hard-won ability that demands massive sacrifices? The ability to move doesn't come without downsides. I don't mean as a speaker; I mean as a life-form.

Consider how easy life is as a plant. Hungry? Grow some food inside your body with sunlight, your chlorophyll, and nutrients from the soil. Thirsty? Suck up some water from the ground. Want to procreate? Drop a seed and let wind, water, and animals do the work for you.

If you're a human, on the other hand, the sacrifices it takes to enable movement are many. Hungry? People have to till soil, plant seeds, wait wait wait, and harvest. Thirsty? Better go search for a clear stream. Looking to pass along your genes? You must find, woo, and mate with a partner. What a lot of work!

Yet moving also gives us the ability to search for food during famine, travel for water in drought, and visit other tribes to find new prospective mates if those nearby don't suit. It's not without its benefits. Given the cost but also the value, why wouldn't you take advantage of what moving can offer?

So if you're able, let's explore walking and talking.

Try this thought experiment: Imagine how your feet move over the course of a sixty-second interaction in which you give a lost tourist directions through your home city. You're walking down the street, moving forward with purpose in a linear direction. The tourist causes a detour in your path with their polite interruption. You stop. Your feet come to a complete rest hip distance apart beneath you. Both feet share the equal burden of your weight to economize effort. You remain still as the tourist asks you a question. Then you shift your feet as you move a bit to stand next to them to see the map from their perspective. Again, your feet come to a complete rest. Once you have ascertained their destination and determined the most convenient route to get there, perhaps your feet move quite a bit more: over to the edge of the curb, for example, to gesture to the next corner where they should turn or back to where they were standing to emphasize the direction from whence they came. Let's say at this point you're in the slightest hurry, as pausing for a minute to give directions increases the chance that you'll miss the train or bus you are aiming to catch. You might even walk backward briefly as you hustle off, your feet moving in reverse toward your destination as you call out the last direction or salutation.

Can you imagine that dance pattern on the floor?

What is the point of this thought experiment, besides acknowledging what a gracious resident you are? In that entire small-scale dance routine, your movement was intentional. And so we come to the rule I offer my clients for movement. As you have perhaps noticed, I don't give many hard-and-fast rules in this book, but I will in this case. Here it is:

WHEN YOU ARE PRESENTING, YOU CAN MOVE AS FAR AS YOU WANT, AS MUCH AS YOU WANT, AND AS OFTEN AS YOU WANT AS LONG AS IT'S INTENTIONAL.

People get so turned around—mentally, I mean, but sometimes even physically—that they forget how to move! They wander, fidget, sway back and forth, pace, do a jazz square, and all other manner of random, needless movement.

That scattered, arbitrary movement is a problem for two reasons. It certainly conveys discomfort to your audience as they try to square the cognitive dissonance of a speaker saying one thing with their words and another with their feet. But worse, it usually unlocks the Vicious Cycle of Bad Communication, where the instability of your feet reinforces the instability of your communication. Your constant, unnecessary movement prohibits your communication from attaining a sense of stability and foundation.

Let me give an example. I once changed a woman's career in four hours. She was a stellar executive, but she struggled with profound stage fright. Whenever she spoke in public, she would get monumentally nervous. She would start the presentation, already grappling with her butterflies, and then within the first thirty seconds she would become painfully aware of how much she was blushing. This awareness of the red in her cheeks would become so obsessional that she would have literally no recollection of what she said, what happened, what the audience said or asked, and what she answered. Often, she couldn't even recollect how she got off the stage.

Although hers was an extreme case, you've likely heard of something similar or even experienced something like this yourself.

She and I got to work. Her first statement was—of course—"I need to stop blushing." If you've been paying even passing attention, you can probably guess that I disabused her of this goal immediately. "Blushing is a symptom," I told her. "The more you try to avoid blushing, the more you will blush. To stop blushing, we must deal with the core matter, which is the muscle-memory pattern that prevents you from focusing on anything besides the hue in your cheeks."

What did we discover? As soon as she began presenting, she would start a subtle but unmistakable pattern that looked like this: She would shift her weight back and forth from one foot to the other and repetitively smooth her hair behind her ears. The repetitive feet shifting fed into a faster rate of speech; the fast rate of speech fed into a shallow pattern of breathing; shallow breathing fed into an inner experience of "drowning"; and the experience of drowning triggered a fight-or-flight reaction that manifested in multiple ways, only one of which was flushed cheeks. The hair tic came from a self-conscious desire to camouflage her red cheeks with her hand motion.

Rather than trying to prevent her cheeks from flushing or having her wear more foundation, we just started with her feet. Instead of telling her to stop shifting the weight back and forth (which would be thought suppression), I knelt and placed a book on top of each foot and told her she needed to speak, but without letting the books slip at all. As silly as that may sound for her brain, it wasn't silly at all for her feet. Ever learn a dance routine? If there is some section you struggle with, you often must slow it down and go through the steps with your feet at half or even quarter speed. Your head doesn't need to learn; your feet do. I was giving her feet the tactile feedback that they needed to recognize the unconscious pattern they were in.

Her feet learned to settle into the floor; she felt far more grounded; when she felt that way, she breathed in before she began speaking, and her rate of speech slowed by about 40 percent; she was more in command of the first thing she said, and she was in her body enough to actually be able to notice what she just said—which was a smart thought! The experience of sharing a smart thought kicked her attention instantly into considering what to say next; in that moment of consideration, she breathed in, her nervous system calmed, her right hand didn't have the need to mask her blushing by smoothing back her hair, and lo and behold, her face didn't flush. After about forty-five seconds of speaking, a huge grin came across her face as she realized she was "public speaking," but without the typical accompanying mortal dread.

She wasn't aware that the simple habit of constantly shifting her weight was triggering an entire pattern. Once she had that awareness and was given the tactile feedback and tools to alter it, she unraveled the pattern like a falling spool of thread.

That story is not to suggest, however, that you must only stay still. Far from it! Back to my **hard-and-fast rule**: You may move whenever you have need, but you must have need. Your need needn't be lofty. All the following needs are absolutely sufficient to merit movement:

- "I need to move across the stage to see others in the audience."
- "I need to move to the projector screen to gesture to a visual."
- "I need to move downstage to create a more intimate dynamic with those in the front row."
- "I need to come out from behind the podium to create a sense of immediacy and spontaneity for my audience."
- "I need to go back behind the podium to check my notes."
- "I need to move to take a drink of water."

That's just a starting list. So this **hard-and-fast rule** is not intended to stymie you but rather to set you free. Artists speak about "freedom within form," the notion that by restricting oneself to a specific form or structure, the restriction itself helps unleash new creativity and variety within an old, time-tested form. So it is with this rule. And this is not the rule because I say so but because this is how communicators move when not thinking about their communication: they move to help their audience understand their message.

Enough explaining, let's get to doing.

I've adapted the exercise you're about to learn from one taught to me by an extraordinary voice and speech teacher named Deb Hecht. When I was studying acting in conservatory, if Deb was trying to help us find a more stable foundation, she would drop down to foot level and—gently, but firmly—"nail" imaginary wooden pegs through our feet and into the floor. She would place one hand on top of one foot at a time and tap-tap-tap that hand with her other, gently transferring the pressure, impact, and vibration from her hand taps into our feet. Once you've become accustomed to this exercise, it's actually a quite pleasant sensation.

Just as I explained about intentional movement, the intention here was not that we could never move but rather that we could move if movement was required. And if we needed to move, we were mandated to peel our feet up off the floor using the requisite effort it would take to pull wooden pegs out of the floor—at which point we were allowed to move elsewhere in the room. But once we arrived at the destination, we had to nail our feet back into the floor—either imaginarily or literally relying once more on Deb to physically tap our feet.

If you want to try this drill right now, you can. You don't need me (or Deb). First, make sure your knees are feeling up to the task of squatting. If not, you can modify this drill using any kind of staff or stick that allows you to gently tap your feet while remaining upright. An umbrella, broom handle, cane, or plastic bat will suffice. It's self-explanatory how to use that tool for the adapted version, so I'll explain the squatting drill in detail, and then if you prefer to modify it, you easily can.

Start by standing. Then practice the squat you just learned in the posture chapter. Now that you have your hands near enough to your feet to do so, tap-tap-tap imaginary wooden pegs into your feet. Go back and forth, alternating between feet, until you have tapped continually for about thirty to forty-five seconds. Now you can stand up. Practice speaking in this position. When you want to move, feel free to do so—as long as it's intentional. In that case, pull your feet up and out of the ground deliberately, imagining you are prying wooden pegs out of the floor. Move for whatever purpose you choose or to whatever destination you need. Once there, you must do the same activity—renail your feet to the floor with those imaginary pegs. Repeat this process each time you want to move. Over time you will quickly build muscle memory and the actual nailing of the imaginary pegs will no longer be necessary.

If you want to use the staff or stick version instead of squatting, just use the end of the staff to tap your feet.

SHOE EXERCISE

Now let's get to the modification I have developed. It relies on shoes, so you'll need to gather a few pairs. Please choose shoes that are stable and well worn (brand-new high heels need not apply for this job). Once you have those in hand, place the pairs in various locations in the room. If it helps, imagine the room is a stage, and you are positioning the shoes in the most advantageous spots where the audience can see you clearly. Then, leaving the shoes where they are, walk to any wall of the room. Now, think of some content you can present. When you have chosen the content, I want you to try the following: Walk to one pair of shoes in silence and stand on top of them. Once you are on the shoes, you can begin speaking your content. As you speak, you must keep your feet stationary. Those shoes represent the onstage positions where you might stand and deliver, and—given that they are not attached to your feet—those shoes won't stay on if you pace, shift, or wander. When you are inclined to move, you can do so. Just step off the shoes, leave them exactly where they are, and move to a different pair. As you move, you may either be silent (living through that luxurious amount of quiet) or continue speaking (as if you were giving a TED talk that is undoubtedly about to go viral). When you arrive at your destination, stand on that pair, ensuring that once you're atop the shoes they do not move. Keep exploring this drill as long as you like, making multiple stops at the various pairs of shoes. Your job is to anchor your feet to the floor whenever you are in a standing position, while enjoying the freedom to move should the spirit move you.

Once you have built muscle memory with this drill, remove the shoes from the floor and continue doing the drill, imagining you are slipping into various pairs at various places on the stage. As you get better and better at intentional movement, notice how you can walk to any point in the room—not just the ones where the shoes, imaginary or not, are stationed—so long as that movement is intentional.

PRACTICE OR PERFORMANCE?

The stance techniques in this chapter are absolutely practice and performance tools. You probably can't sprinkle flour or place pairs of multiple shoes all over your office floor. But you can come close by exploring some of the following. If you are giving a presentation while standing, wear a pair of shoes that reminds you to ground your feet and move with intentionality. If you have access to the space beforehand, you can even walk the potential pathways you might use. Choose places where your feet can come to stillness and maybe even reach down and draw an imaginary outline of your feet in those places. Or grab a book, put it on the floor in that location, and briefly stand on it to reignite the muscle memory of standing on this book. Find creative ways to remind your feet that they know how to do both essential skills of this chapter: (1) remain still; and (2) move with purpose.

If it gives you courage, consider how actors and news reporters use versions of these same techniques. Stage actors are accustomed to walking through imaginary structures, the floor plan of which is indicated with tape on the floor. Theatrical productions often come together with multiple departments building their contributions simultaneously. So the actors are rehearsing at the same time that the costume designer (and team) is sewing and creating the costumes; the lighting designer (and team) is building the lighting plot; and the set designer (and team) is building the set. Therefore, if actors want to get a sense of the theatrical world they'll be inhabiting but those other departments haven't completed their work yet, they rely on a few physical aids. Costume designers often provide the performance shoes early in the process so actors can explore how their character stands and moves in them. Similarly, the stage manager (and team) often place variously colored masking tape on the rehearsal room floor to precisely mark out the floor plan of the structures that will eventually be the set. The measurements on these blueprints are very accurate and detailed—even including indication of stairs and differently colored tape to map out second or third floors.

News reporters and film actors sometimes place an X mark on the floor with tape or some other kind of physical prop (a wooden crate, a line in the sand, etc.) to indicate where they need to stand to deliver a line or wrap up the end of an on-location bit of reporting. In both instances, the set needs to be crafted to provide the audience the most compelling scene. Imagine the scene: For the film example, the actor must move into the right lighting angle, with the ideal background visible or obscured, and assume the perfect eyeline with the camera to achieve the director's vision. When doing a "walk-and-talk," a news reporter needs to find the right position in the shot to highlight the activity happening behind them as well the right endpoint that lights them effectively, creates a "button" for the story, and occupies the frame with the correct balance and ratio. In both cases, the physical props help the speakers accomplish their job—and hopefully do it in fewer takes so the crew can move onto the next scene or story.

So steal a page out of the actor's and news reporter's playbook and find ways to take control of the spaces where you perform. And use the tools in this chapter to do so.

WHAT ABOUT VIRTUAL?

When communicating virtually, stance is slightly less relevant for your audience for an obvious reason: People can't see your feet (or whether you're continuously moving them). But it might still be profoundly relevant for you. Even if constant (but obscured) movement isn't problematic for the audience's sake, it probably is undermining your ability to experience ease, calm, and stability. Remember the example of the professional who frequently blushed and even more frequently moved her feet? That movement was undermining her ability to unlock the Virtuous Cycle of Good Communication.

The incredible liberation that virtual communication offers here is that you can completely modify your space to assist your feet, and your audience will be none the wiser. If you want to go to the nth degree and you have a floor that can be easily cleaned, try the flour tool. Or stand on the pages of this book. Or even put strong, double-sided tape under the soles of your feet or shoes. See what benefit you can realize when you give your feet unmistakable real-time physical resistance to movement.

If you're typically seated for video calls, first consider standing at times! But for seated calls, posture is more relevant than stance because the chair is your foundation, not your feet. Swivel chairs can present a risk, of course, and repetitive swiveling is a distant cousin of constant foot movement. But for the most part, stance isn't the most important focus when sitting. So if you want to remind yourself about the more essential areas of physical presence when working remotely, flip back one chapter and review the posture chapter or quickly finish this sentence and move on to Chapter 15, which focuses on gestures.

CHAPTER 15

PHYSICAL PRESENCE
PART THREE: GESTURES

How to Stop Obsessing About Your Hands

teach public speaking and communication skills around the world. I coach the faculty at Columbia Business School, including two deans. I have coached presidential candidates on debate prep, media training, on-camera skills, stump speeches, and more. I work with blue-chip organizations like the National Football League, Major League Baseball, New York University Law School, and many others. I drop my bio in this discussion not to focus on me but on you. In all those environments, what do you ask me the most? You guessed it. You—the royal you, meaning all the people I coach and teach—ask me, "What should I do with my hands?"

Why is this the most frequent question? It's not because it's the most important part of your communication. It is simply because most of the coaching people receive about gestures consists of a litany of negative adjustments, a textbook example of how thought suppression is not useful. Test this. Write down one of the don'ts that you have heard about hand gestures.

"Don't_____

_____

_____."

Most likely you've written down something like:

+ Don't make distracting hand gestures.
+ Don't click your pen.
+ Don't play with your ring.
+ Don't point at your audience.
+ Don't keep your hands behind your back.
+ Don't put your hands under the table.
+ Don't put your hands in your pockets.
+ Don't cross your arms.
+ Don't gesture too low.
+ Don't gesture too high.
+ Don't make gestures that are too dramatic.
+ Don't clasp your hands.
+ Don't touch your face.
+ Don't cover your mouth with your hands.

Those are just the first ones that come to mind. With all those don'ts, I defy you to say what you should *do* with your hands.

Why is it that we get so many don'ts about our hand gestures? One reason is because it's an easy thing to pick on. Nonexperts observe someone communicating, and they don't necessarily have a specific thing to share that is tremendously insightful. But they've heard others critique gestures, and they can notice gestures. So, they say, "Don't make distracting hand gestures."

It's not their fault—they're trying to be helpful. They just may not have more instructive or useful things to say.

However, it turns out that this coaching is highly problematic because not only does it activate thought suppression ("Don't think about..."), but also, in this case, the advice—were one able to achieve it—isn't even good!

If you were talking to someone who didn't speak your native language, would you use gestures? You better believe it. If you were helping a lost tourist find a destination, would you use gestures? You better believe it.

THE SOURCE OF GESTURES

Where do gestures come from? They don't come from a communication specialist's recommendation; they come from a deep human need to use every part of our communication instrument to make certain our audience understands unmistakably what we're saying and how we feel about it. I know—from years of doing this with tens of thousands of people—that the following is true: In tremendously other-focused situations, you probably use your hand gestures more than you realize. You might even know that to be true. But that knowledge by itself might feel hard to accept to the degree you need to unleash more gestural freedom and ease.

That is a phrase you'll read multiple times in this chapter: Gesture with freedom and ease. I've chosen that phrase very specifically. To the extent that "don't make distracting hand gestures" has attached itself to your gray matter like the tangled tendrils of a toxic vine on a tree, I humbly suggest you replace that phrase with "use gestures with freedom and ease."

Why that phrase? Because that's what we're after. We're not searching for more gestures in general. Neither are we searching for identical, repetitive gestures. We're looking to unlock how you gesture when you are not thinking about how you gesture.

That litany of don'ts is not the only way gesture coaching goes wrong. Let's say you have miraculously avoided that thought-suppression minefield and actually received a "do." What might that sound like? Probably something like "Keep your gestures within a safe zone," or "Use a home base and come back to it repeatedly." These bits of advice are so well traveled you may recognize them. More obscure ones may be new to you. I once encountered students being advised to "keep a beach ball aloft." They dutifully floated their hands aimlessly.

Politicians at the highest level even receive this type of coaching. I know for a fact that a famous one was counseled to make a repeated "command gesture" that involved holding their hands and fingers in a specific way. The problem? Their audience saw yet one more politician on autopilot, doing the same repetitive gesture as though on communication cruise control. And this politician received the kiss-of-death label: inauthentic.

CHAPTER 15
GESTURES

These suggestions possess the same flaw as the other reductive, arbitrary feedback you've learned about in *Don't Say Um*, such as "hold eye contact for eight to twelve seconds" and "speak in a low, even voice to project gravitas."

Gesture zones and home bases are examples of lacquered-on, one-size-fits-all advice that creates disconnected, generic communicators—speakers who use less of themselves, not more, and who look like every other bland, hesitant presenter droning mindlessly in front of an audience.

Instead of the thought-suppression don'ts and the reductive do's, your challenge in this book—and my job as your guide—is to unlock the only sources of gestures that have real value: you and the audience to whom you're speaking.

So, for the third time in this book, we're going to explore Silent Storytelling. The first time we used it to unlock vocal variety; the second, we examined eye contact and its source. Now its purpose is to make your gestures as eloquent as your words. What does that mean? Is this about doing charades? No, you're simply going to use your gestures with as much freedom and ease as you can to communicate your point. How? Let's first use that drill you already know (and hopefully love) to unleash more freedom and ease with your gestures, and then we'll look at how to escape one specific negative habit if you have formed it.

DRILL 1: ONCE MORE, WITH FEELING: SILENT STORYTELLING FOR GESTURES

As for the drill you already know, the first stage of this exploration is a fun reveal. Remember when I told you to save the video footage you took of yourself in Chapter 9 on vocal variety when you first tried Silent Storytelling? We're going to watch that footage again. If you have deleted the footage or simply can't find it, fear not. We'll navigate to new terrain shortly. But if you still have access to the footage, we'll watch it shortly. Last time I asked you to observe your vocal variety and note how the exercise helped unlock more of it. Now you have a simpler task. I just want you to watch the footage and see what you think of your gestures. If you're like most of the people I coach, you might think that the extremity of the exercise yields a few gestures that are overkill—a level that is simply artificial compared to how you typically speak, even at your most other-focused best. But just as likely, you'll also think that most of the footage is shockingly…good! The exaggerated gestures that Silent Storytelling requires might be 10 percent too much, but they're not 10× too much. And you may be surprised to see that you prefer your communication when you're silently storytelling compared to when not.

So, pop some corn, put your feet up, and watch the footage you recorded during the Silent Storytelling activity in Chapter 9.

* * *

What did you think? Surprising? Let's keep going.

Regardless of whether you have (and viewed) your previous footage, you'll need some new content for this exercise. I want you to think of two topics. The first is some professional content you can speak about for five to ten minutes, because we'll be starting and stopping within the topic. The second is any of these three examples of personal content: an outdoor adventure story, an epic nightmare commuting story, or a bit of how-to instructions for a hands-on activity you like (cooking, gardening, building, coding, origami, painting, etc.).

I want you to deliver both pieces of content twice. First, you'll record yourself sharing both pieces of content without Silent Storytelling; then you'll do it with it. Remember: You need to hold yourself to a high standard. Make sure you do not record four kinds of identical footage. That would be an indication that you were not, in fact, Silent Storytelling at all. It is your sacred duty in this exercise to go as far as necessary with your facial expressions, enunciation, and gestural life to ensure that an observer could understand your content without the benefit of sound.

The flow is as follows. Don't watch any of your footage until you've completed all four. First, film yourself telling your professional content without the exercise. In other words, just talk as you normally would. Next, tell your personal content, also without the exercise. Then, do the professional content, but while doing Silent Storytelling. Last, do the personal content while Silent Storytelling. Once you're done, please watch all four clips.

Before you start, if you need a refresh, this is what you learned about Silent Storytelling in Chapter 9 on vocal variety:

In this drill, you are allowed to communicate to an audience using all of yourself except your voice. The idea is to use all your communication instrument as expressively as needed to help an audience understand precisely what you're saying, even without the benefit of sound. That means you will need to: (1) (silently) enunciate your words so expressively that a listener might be able to read your lips; (2) gesture with sufficient expressiveness and specificity that a listener might understand where/when/who/how by watching the story your hands are telling; and (3) allow your facial expressions to vary and reflect the ups/downs, ins/outs, and lefts/rights of your content. To clarify, this is not charades: You do not need to act out the content or indicate the number of words or syllables. Just think of this as turning up the volume on every aspect of your communication because you can't turn up the volume on the sound.

Ready? Go and film. Once you're done, watch all four segments.

*   *   *

First, did you satisfactorily do the Silent Storytelling exercise? If the footage from all four segments looks identical—the same range of hand gestures, facial expressions, and enunciation, even though some had sound and some didn't—you did not go far enough with the drill. If that's the case, do not keep reading. Go back, do the exercise again, and this time nudge yourself further to embrace the drill! Once you've done that, watch again. If it's still identical, push yourself to go further, yet again. You're not done until the clips look quite different. At this point in the book, I'm quite confident your Silent Storytelling is in fact sufficiently expansive to experience its benefit, but the reason I'm perhaps overemphasizing the quality control here is that I want to ensure you're adjusting the right things and extracting the maximal benefit of each exercise.

You have four clips you just viewed. Here's the million-dollar question: Which did you prefer? Which version of you seemed the best to take to a cocktail party? To lead a remote or hybrid meeting? To accept a lifetime achievement award? To interview someone or be interviewed? For most people, sadly, the only clip of the four they would not want to bring to any of the aforementioned communication scenarios is the version of themselves speaking on their professional content as they typically would. But the happy news is that you likely just saw three clips of what "better" can look like. If in fact you preferred your first video to the other three, hurrah! That means one of two things: (1) gestures may not be an area of improvement you need to explore; and (2) you've already made significant progress in this book and your gestures are operating with more freedom and ease than they were lo those many pages ago.

DRILL 2: BALL THROWING FOR GESTURES

Remember the ball-throwing exercise we did for stance, where you threw a ball at the wall and tried to keep your feet anchored to a single position as you did so? As promised, we're going to revisit it now, but this time focused on gestures. This exercise is intended to break the muscle memory you may have built of clutching your hands or imposing reductive constraints like "don't use distracting hand gestures" and "keep your gestures in a safe zone."

Start by doing the ball-throwing activity again. Once you've done it enough to refamiliarize yourself with the exercise, you're going to alternate between throwing and not throwing. But when you pause the throwing activity, you must retain the same level of free and varied arm movement that you did when catching the ball at all angles—because now we're focused on gestures.

Here it is step-by-step:

- Do the ball-throwing drill again (detailed in Chapter 14).
- Once you're in a flow, catch the ball, retain it in your catching hand, and talk with gestures and movements as expressive as those throws and catches.
- Shift back and forth between throwing and not throwing enough times to make the freedom of arm and hand movement similar in both modes.

The last stage of the drill is to put the ball down but retain the muscle-memory benefit of the drill. Holding the ball in one hand while talking tends to help people remember to allow gestural freedom, but you can't lead meetings or give speeches holding a ball unless you're using it as a prop in a relevant way for your content. So, once you've really got this drill down, put the ball down during the nonthrowing sections, but keep your "freedom and ease" gestures alive and moving.

If throwing and catching is challenging for you (no judgment!), scrap the real ball and just do the exercise using an imaginary energy ball. The purpose of this drill is not to improve your fine motor skills and coordination, so I don't want your focus overwhelmingly occupied with the challenging act of catching a rebounding ball. If you do the imaginary energy ball version, though, it is more difficult to execute the drill with discipline. People tend to be lazy and general with their throws. If you go the imaginary route, it is your gravest ethical requirement to imaginarily throw it accurately to a specific spot and use an exaggerated amount of arm extension to catch precisely at the exact rebound location.

If you haven't already tried the drill at this point, please go do so, in each of its progressions.

* * *

Well done! I'm certain you noticed greater freedom in moving your arms and hands, but did you also notice your feet? Have they become more comfortable being stationary since last chapter? Hopefully so. Either way, this drill is a great way to remind your feet that they can stay still.

As I mentioned, let's now move on to one specific negative gestural habit you may have. It's one of the most common limiting patterns: clasping. In the ball-throwing drill we just did, what else might you have noticed? For those claspers out there, did you notice how holding the ball prevented you from going into that habitual contraction? You know who you are: You have developed a security blanket or home base position where you bring your hands together in some type of stationary pose whenever you're presenting. You may have even been coached deliberately to develop this position, to find a calming central base to return your hands to whenever in doubt about how to use them. That looks different for different people:

fingers knitted together tightly; palms placed together in a prayer pose; fingertips delicately touching; hands pointed downward in an inverted triangle. If you don't have this habit, the previous four descriptions might be slightly mystifying. If you do, you know exactly what I'm talking about.

Why am I depriving you of your security blanket? You worked so hard to develop something to do to occupy your hands; you may have even received coaching to do so and/or feel satisfied and dignified while doing it. Why on earth would I try to abolish it? Because you probably don't do it in real life. That's why.

Remember the Little League sports team example? When giving that team an inter-inning speech, you wouldn't clasp your hands the entire time in an effort to convey some sort of contrived gravitas. If you were walking a friend through some recommendations about how to get their life back on track, you wouldn't retreat to your calcified clasped position. Why do you do it when presenting, then? It's not natural; it's habitual. And that's reason one why I want you to question it and then develop some other choices.

Reason two is even more crucial: Far from keeping you safe—providing a home base, a safe port in the storm, or some other visual metaphor—it may be putting you in danger. Danger of what, you might ask? The danger of not communicating at your best! The danger of unwittingly unleashing the Vicious Cycle of Bad Communication, when your delivery makes your content weaker and your entire communication instrument contracts in lockstep.

Let me share a story to illustrate. It's the origin story of the drill you're about to learn. I once worked with a client (we'll call her Nancy) who had a habit of clasping her hands—not when she spoke, mind you, but when she presented. If you spoke with her impromptu, when she wasn't delivering a formal talk, she used her hands fluidly and frequently. But as soon as the word *presentation* entered the room, she would clasp her hands together in a misguided attempt to "not distract the audience."

You know what is distracting? Watching someone strive to not move their hands. But when she presented, that was the sole focus of her attention. She was endeavoring to portray a calm, centered, dignified persona, and the linchpin for that persona was keeping her hands as still as stone. But in real life Nancy moved her hands. So restricting that movement led to a whole series of unnatural patterns: She would clasp her hands tightly, even to the point of twisting and straining her fingers; the tension would move up her arms, tighten her shoulders, restrict the movement of her ribs, and diminish the size of her inhale. You've read far enough in this book to recognize that all those physical maladjustments are telltale signs that she was in the midst of a vicious cycle. Predictably, her content would fall apart and her nerves skyrocket.

Also predictably, it wasn't sufficient to ask her to stop clasping her hands; when I did that, she agreed to the request, and then—as I knew she would—reverted right back to the habit. So I crumpled up a ball of paper, positioned it in between her clasped hands, and said, "This is a puffer fish on the bottom of the ocean. Feel its sharp spines stabbing into your palms? Say, 'Ow, ow, ow!'" She held the crumpled paper and cried out in faux pain. "Do it again," I asked; more fish holding and faux cries. "A third time," I said. She did the activity again. "Now, put the paper aside and begin delivering your presentation, but if your hands come back together, the flesh on your palms is going to be impaled by the excruciating spikes of an inflated puffer fish." She began speaking. The ancient muscle memory of clasping brought her hands together, but when her fingertips touched, she was able to instantly bounce her hands back open. She proceeded to talk for several minutes with her hands unclasped.

For some clients, even the puffer fish exercise isn't sufficient to change the habit. For those folks, we go one step further and enlist the use of an exercise band. I loop the band around their arms and torso at elbow level. I instruct them to talk and gesture but to keep continual pressure on the band. They can stretch it wider to make points or use gestures, but they're not permitted to let the band have slack in it. The intensity of this activity and the tactile feedback it provides are finally enough for them to experience a different possibility.

Nancy didn't need the exercise band; the puffer fish drill worked—and not only in the way you might think. Yes, it eradicated the clasp. But it also unlocked other miraculous changes in her communication: Suddenly, her feet were stable on the ground; her shoulders dropped; her tummy released; her gaze centered; her voice practically exploded with more resonance. Liberating her hands to move rather than clasp liberated her entire body to breathe, stand, and move as freely as she might do when talking to a friend over food.

I don't know what your clasping habits are or are not. Given the extremity of her habit, it's unlikely you are equally plagued by clasping. But if Nancy's story feels familiar and the positive result impossible, take a page out of my book and try the exercise. Literally. Tear out the following page—which just so happens to have a picture of an inflated spiny puffer fish—and try the same exercise that Nancy did. There's only one rule: Talk, and as you do, your hands can do anything they want so long as they don't come together and impale themselves on the fish. And if you need to dial up the level of difficulty, get an exercise band or loop of elastic ribbon or fabric and try the more intense variation.

CHAPTER 15
GESTURES

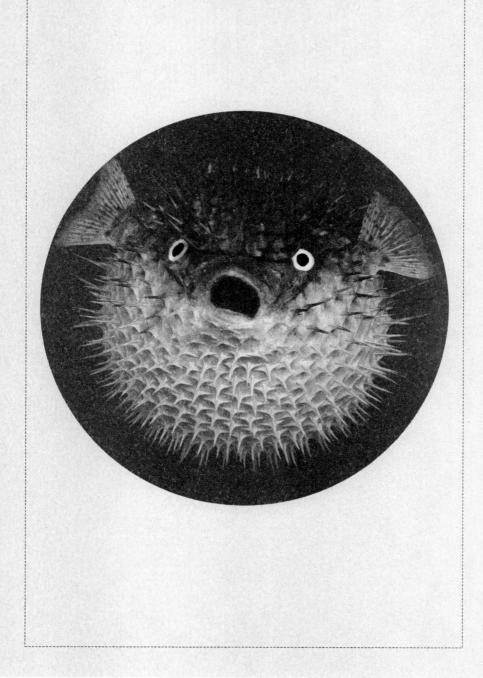

When she wasn't self-focused, Nancy moved her hands so much more than she thought. That realization and the drill transformed her communication life. How much do you move your hands when you're not self-focused? That is the ultimate question you get to investigate, the answer to which may well set you free.

PRACTICE OR PERFORMANCE?

For this chapter and the topic of gestures, I'm going to ask you to blur the distinction between practice and performance. Can you throw balls at a wall or hold a crumpled-up piece of "puffer fish" paper when speaking to an audience? Unlikely. But can you consciously try to take on the size of expressivity that Silent Storytelling, the ball exercise, and the puffer fish technique encourage? Definitely! So use those exercises to practice, but then try to fearlessly integrate the changes they yield into real-life scenarios.

WHAT ABOUT VIRTUAL?

I give only one caveat about the "distracting hand gestures" topic. There's one place where this hyperfocus on "what not to do with your gestures" is relevant—on camera. And it's not because you shouldn't make "distract-ing" hand gestures on camera. In fact, if you watch a lively roundtable on a TV talk show or listen to a group of panelists discuss an issue, not only will you see free and frequent gestures, but as an audience member you will probably appreciate them—in large part because the TV personality who is using gestures is probably using more vocal variety, crisper enunci-ation, and more facial expressiveness as well.

The reason to be mindful is this: The size of the frame and the angle of the camera determine what your audience sees. To the viewer, you're appear-ing in an arbitrarily sized box. They might only see the upper half of your torso, in which case your hands may repetitively leave and enter the frame. If it's a close-up, they might not see your hands at all. If your camera and com-puter are positioned lower, your hands might seem disproportionately large, their proximity to the camera making them appear outsized.

But this does not mean the speaker should not gesture. It does mean the speaker should understand the size of the frame and get accustomed to how gestures work in that context. The good news is the world of remote work has made this learning curve less steep. Very likely you have multiple opportunities each week to experiment with the camera angle and size of the frame. So don't you dare give yourself ridiculous, unactionable, and self-critical feedback like "don't use distracting hand gestures on camera." Instead, treat yourself like the nuanced, sophisticated communicator you are and—like a scientist—research what your audience perceives. Remember: Technology is there to serve you; you are not there to serve technology. So move the computer around, change the setup of your work position, and center yourself in the frame in such a way that you're able to gesture with freedom and ease rather than focusing on not using "distracting hand gestures."

Even in that situation, there are only a very few gestures that are strictly forbidden. The most egregious is also the most obvious: Don't put your hands right in front of the camera, because your hand is not invisible. We need to see you. Also, refrain from putting your hand in front of your mouth unless you're politely covering a yawn (better yet, save the yawns for the vocal warm-up in the next chapter and keep them out of your remote meeting!). These rules are not important because violating them constitutes a Hand Gesture Sin but because we will have a harder time seeing and hearing you.

On to the fun stuff that virtual communication unlocks for gestures. I'll share three tools here.

One, if you happen to be on audio only (either on the phone or on a video call without camera), force yourself to use your hands much more expressively than you might have previously. No one can see you, so go for it! Then notice how much more vocal variety and expressivity you use. Remember: your voice is your body.

Two, if you're on camera, you can still use the Silent Storytelling and other gestural tools from this chapter. If clasping is an issue for you, take advantage of the Cloak of Invisibility and keep your crumpled paper puffer fish right on your desk (but below the camera's view) to remind yourself to open your hands. You can do the same thing with the ball exercise—keep the prop on your desk as a reminder.

Three, if you want to modify the Silent Storytelling drill, do so in the following way. Instead of being silent (which you can't—people need and want to hear you!), shift the focus slightly and challenge yourself to keep your hands in the frame the entire call. Try this on low-consequence calls. It will feel very awkward at first—and might even appear a bit strange. But you're doing it for a very important reason—to normalize the experience of using your hands as much as you do "in real life." Once you've forced yourself to go to that extreme level of activity, scale it back to 50 percent...then maybe even 40 or 30 percent. Soon you'll find the right level that feels familiar. It *should* feel familiar after all. It's you! But just a more conversational and other-focused version of you.

*   *   *

With the exercises you've learned and awareness you've gained in this fifteenth chapter of *Don't Say Um*, you get to embark on a new chapter in your communication life, a chapter that starts with the tantalizing question: "What should I do with my attention, now that I no longer have to obsess about my hands?"

For starters, we can train your attention on the next part of *Don't Say Um*, where you'll learn how to warm up, how to navigate nerves, how to recover, and how to retain the lessons you've learned. Let's get to Part Three.

CHAPTER 15
GESTURES

EVERYTHING YOU NEED TO GET READY, RECOVER, AND RETAIN

CHAPTER 16

WARMING UP

How to Get Ready (and Stop Obsessing About Your Script)

Over the next four chapters, I am going to give you practical tools to: (1) prepare; (2) navigate nerves; (3) handle mistakes; and (4) retain the skills you've learned in *Don't Say Um*. I'm grouping these skill areas together because they are essential to set yourself up for success and keep that success rolling.

PREPARING

It all starts with preparing well. Right?

Not in this book. What I want to focus on isn't how to thoroughly prepare or avoid procrastination.

I won't talk about that because you probably already know that. You already know you should prepare extensively and avoid procrastinating. You should definitely do both those things. For real. I imagine you don't; I hope you do. But either way, I have no interest in repeating the same stuff you already know or attempting to guilt you into doing what you chronically don't do.

What I do want to focus on is changing how you prepare. I want to make it faster, freer, and more intuitive. And my grand goal is that you will actually prepare (rather than procrastinate) because of these improvements and prepare in the right way.

People make three frequent mistakes in their prep: They generate their content primarily by writing, not speaking; once they have their content, they fail to practice out loud; and they don't warm up. Let's look at each.

People Create Content Primarily by Writing, Not Speaking

A speech isn't a white paper to be handed out to an audience; it is made up of spoken words shared by a speaker with listeners. To craft content that sounds more like how people talk instead of how they write, try something I call Out Loud Drafting. It is exactly what it sounds like: You draft what you're going to say by speaking it out loud rather than writing it first. To do this, simply give yourself an open-ended prompt to kick you off. Here are some good ones:

- What am I trying to communicate with this talk?
- What is the main idea I want people to remember from my talk?
- If my talk were a movie trailer, what would come next after "In a world…"?

Those are a few example questions to get you going, but make up others on your own. Use open-ended questions (*what*, *how*, and *why* are good starting words to ensure that). Ask questions out loud, and then actually speak the answers. Do the activity three or four times, getting clearer and clearer on your message. Once you've done that, then you can write down some of the ideas you've discovered. You can even do the activity while recording or transcribing yourself so technology captures what you say.

Out Loud Drafting improves the preparation process for most people in three ways.

1. It leads to content that sounds like speaking rather than writing. Word choice tends to be more vivid, more monosyllabic,

and less filled with jargon; grammatical construction tends to feature shorter sentences.

2. It helps speakers internalize—or memorize, if necessary— content more easily and faster. By saying it out loud several times in its embryonic form before ever finalizing the content, speakers memorize the flow of argument and internal logic rather than word-for-word passages.

3. It builds a muscle-memory experience of ease and experimentation rather than adrenaline and performance.

They Don't Practice Out Loud

This is a different point from the first. If point one is about figuring out what you want to say by talking it out, this point is about practicing that content—out loud! Speed-reading it under your breath or silently reading it over countless times doesn't count. You have to say the stuff out loud. This point doesn't need extrapolation; it just needs execution.

They Don't Warm Up

Once you know what you're going to say and you've practiced it, do some physical and vocal exercises to get ready. By *warming up*, I don't mean "going through your materials a couple times." I also don't mean "talking to some people beforehand just to make sure you don't have morning voice." What I mean is a physical and vocal warm-up that awakens and primes the human communication instrument for performance. If your body is a musical instrument—as we explored in Chapter 11 on breathing—it stands to reason that instrument should be warmed up and prepared to play.

The most familiar warm-up exercises most people know are tongue twisters: "Peter Piper picked...," "Red Leather, Yellow Leather," and so forth. Tongue twisters are an absolutely essential ritual in improving your day-to-day communication skills as well as your performance in high-consequence situations. I will share some of my favorites later in this chapter, and you can also find those and more at dontsayum.com. These nonsensical phrases, poems, and sentences are so well-known in the theatrical and performance community that I don't even know the original source for many of them. Most I learned when I was in acting conservatory. If you feel like being creative, though, make some up on your own! The final two I have listed were invented by my daughter and wife, respectively. And if you really want to be ambitious, one source takes tongue twisters to the next level: the children's book *Fox in Sox* by Dr. Seuss is the gold standard.

But before I show you specific tongue twisters and other warm-up exercises, I want to give you a warning: If you do this right, it will feel silly. Even with the previous paragraph's emphasis on the importance of warming up, you may be slightly dreading it or ridiculing it in your mind: "I'm going to do a physical and vocal warm-up?! Unlikely." Go ahead and have that thought fully because—as you know very well from this book—humans are bad at thought suppression. Now that you've fully indulged that thought, we can move on to the work of embracing the tool and making it part of your daily communication and presence regimen.

Take a lesson from athletes. As we have explored ad nauseam, speaking is practically a sport. You wouldn't play a competitive sport without spending at least a little time warming up. Athletes warm up; communicators should too.

The activities of a speaking warm-up versus a sports one are very different. The vocal warm-ups you're about to learn are the same things that world-class speakers do—religious leaders, politicians, news anchors, and more. I once was on a panel with a famous news anchor most readers of this book would recognize. When asked a question about her prep, she told the audience about the tongue twisters she learned in her undergraduate theater education that she still does to this day. What's more, I coached a different news anchor you would also recognize. We expanded the warm-up he was doing. Before he goes on air for his evening broadcast, he does the same "silly" exercises you're about to learn.

The presence benefits from warming up are immediate, and you'll get the good health benefit of moving your body more too! I'll let you in on a little secret: I warm up every single workday. I've been in multiple fields of professional communications for more than two decades; I like to think I'm fairly effective at using my voice and body to say stuff to achieve stuff. Does that mean I can kick back at this point? No. Warming up is a daily way to strive to become a stronger communicator. I don't do it for nerves—though it's an excellent way to energize your body and dispel the physical manifestation of nerves. I do it because I know my ability to help others is intimately connected to my ability to say words. Warming up gets my body and voice ready to do that.

And sometimes it's even more than once every workday. Some days I warm up multiple times. The warm-ups might be lightning quick, just thirty seconds of tongue twisters before a lecture or a quick sun salutation to reinvigorate my body before an important call. Stage actors do this; typical Broadway shows feature a pair of two-show days each week (usually, Wednesdays and Saturdays have both matinees and evening shows). Most actors warm up extensively before the 2:00 or 3:00 p.m. matinee show, especially given that their default muscle memory is accustomed to nighttime performances. But then they also do a brief reset warm-up before the second show. They don't need to do an extensive warm-up because their voices and bodies have already been very active. But they do a brief one just to get primed for the day's second show.

For the time being, though, let's focus on at least once a day. Then over time you might expand it to multiple, brief warm-ups two or even three times a day. When will you find a moment to do a communication warm-up every single day? Perhaps it's first thing in the morning when you're taking a shower; in the restroom once you get to work; in a conference room before the day's first meeting; at home before logging on to your first remote call—anywhere. If your day-to-day occurs in less business-centric locations, choose places relevant to you.

And now for a cheat! Cell phones make warming up anywhere more feasible. If you have a cell phone, you have camouflage to warm up without looking odd. Just go outside or walk down the hall and sneakily speak some tongue twisters and vocal exercises into your phone as though you were talking to someone on the other end of the line. No one will be the wiser. If you're feeling even more brazen, do the same thing but just with earbuds.

What should you do in your warm-up? Following is a QR code for the warm-up video library my company, GK Training, posts for our clients (you can also find them at gktraining.com/warm-ups). If you don't feel like using a QR code, I'll also share the instructions for some of the greatest hits right here. Fair warning though: Following along with the videos is the better tool. I've tried my best to accurately describe the movements and activities that follow. But just as it would be hard to comprehend how to swing a golf club solely through written instructions, reading these warm-up instructions is a less-than-ideal way to learn this regimen. Don't believe me? Try to learn a golf backswing with this: "Address the ball; begin to draw your arms back and up, keeping your right upper arm (if right-handed) snugged closely to your rib cage, while your right wrist begins to cock back, and your torso rotates slowly."

If you know an athletic, dance, or martial arts warm-up that you like, use it. That's a great start. Alone, though, it's not sufficient. Compared to a communication warm-up, sports routines spend more time than is needed focused on limbs, which are not the primary engine of communicating. For speaking, on the other hand, a warm-up needs to involve your torso, face, breath, and mouth.

WARM UP THE BODY: TIME TO STRETCH!

Make your body as wide as possible, stretching out in both directions like you are holding the world's biggest beach ball. Stretch your face by opening your mouth and eyes wide and even yawn or say "Ah" as you do. Then do the reverse: Make yourself small and tight in a little crunched ball, squeezing and tensing all muscles, and while you do, mush your face around a little bit. Then feel the relief of stretching out wide again, with the yawn and sound. Repeat this three times until you feel a real muscle release throughout. Breathe as you do this activity.

Reach to three points in the room, alternating your left and right hand at each stage. First reach straight up toward the ceiling, alternating your right and left arms. As you do this, feel the stretch in your ribs and torso, not your arm and shoulder. Do this multiple times. Next, alternately reach toward the corner of the ceiling and the wall on the right and left sides of the room. Reach across your body so your left arm is moving in front of your face and torso to reach toward the seam between the ceiling and right wall of the room. Then do the opposite for your right arm to the left corner of the wall and ceiling. Do this several times also. Then do the same alternating motion but laterally so that your arm is reaching toward the middle side of the opposite wall, basically parallel to the floor. Again, do it multiple times, back and forth. Last, do the same alternating flow but reaching across your body to the seam where the opposite wall meets the floor. Do this a number of times. To keep your breath flowing, yawn throughout this exercise. You will have to force that a bit at the start of the exercise, but as you continue it will happen naturally.

If you know how to do a sun salutation in yoga, do it. That activity is complex enough that if you want to learn how I will simply refer you to the warm-up videos page at dontsayum.com.

WARM UP THE FACE: TIME TO BE A CLOWN!

This first activity requires clean hands. Provided yours are, put your hands on your face and give your face a gentle, thorough massage. Keep your palms pressed against your face and move all the skin of your face around as though you were gently kneading delicious cookie dough.

Next imagine you have been buried in sand at the beach (ideally by loved ones, not bullies!) and a bothersome fly keeps landing on your face. Make the fly leave its perch by moving your face as much as possible: Blow air up toward your face to get the imaginary fly off; wiggle your brow, cheeks, and lips as much as you can; squint and scrunch up your nose. Keep that fly from landing on you!

CHAPTER 16
WARMING UP

Finally, push your lips out as far as they can go in front of your face, making what feels like exaggerated "fishy lips." Pinch your lips together over and over again as though you are giving tiny fish kisses to your fish friends and neighbors.

WARM UP THE BREATH: YAWN ALONG!

The famous Russian acting teacher Konstantin Stanislavski recommended yawning as one of the primary warm-up activities for his actors. Yawning relaxes the throat muscles, lifts the soft palate, and brings breath deeply and naturally into the lungs. It primes you for communication and physically relaxes you at the same time. And if you don't have to yawn? Fake it. If you fake a yawn a few times, you will naturally begin to trigger organic ones. Try this series: Yawn three times. Next: Yawn three times while stretching all your limbs in an expansive, free-form way as if you were lazily preparing to get out of bed on a Sunday morning. Next: yawn three times, but this time endeavor to keep the very tip of your tongue anchored to the roof of your mouth (you will fail but try to anyway!).

Provided you continued to breathe during these body and face warm-ups—and that you breathe while you do the tongue twisters that are coming up next—that's sufficient as a breath warm-up. But breath is such a powerful aspect of our communication that I dedicated an entire chapter (Chapter 11) to it and will also revisit it as a way to navigate nerves in the next chapter. So feel free to refer to those two chapters for more breath focus.

WARM UP THE ARTICULATORS: TIME TO TALK!

Warm up your mouth, lips, tongue, and soft palate with tongue twisters. Fully commit to forming and articulating each word, almost in an exaggerated way. Failure with tongue twisters is sacrificing accuracy for speed. Don't race through these. There is such a thing as a fast and worthless warm-up. If you fly through tongue twisters at a breakneck speed and fumble many of your consonants, all you've warmed up is your tendency to enunciate with mediocrity. Say them as slowly as needed to do them flawlessly, but as quickly as possible, while moving your articulators in as dynamic, extreme, and flexible a way as possible.

Do each of these multiple times and spend five to ten minutes total. Your mouth should be feeling dynamically alive by the time you stop.

+ "The big black bug bit the big black bear, and the big black bear bled blue-black blood."
+ "Topeka, topeka, topeka, topeka. Bodega, bodega, bodega, bodega. Topeka, bodega, topeka, bodega, topeka, bodega, topeka, bodega. Bodega, topeka, bodega, topeka, bodega, topeka, bodega, topeka."
+ "Will you wait, will you wait, will you wait, will you wait? Will you wait for Willie and Winnie Williams?"
+ "Paper poppy, baby bubble, paper poppy, baby bubble. Paper poppy, paper poppy, baby bubble, baby bubble."
+ "You know New York; you need New York; you know you need unique New York."
+ "Whether the weather be hot or whether the weather be cold, we'll weather the weather, whatever the weather, whether we're young or we're old. Whether the weather be cold or whether the weather be hot, we'll weather the weather, whatever the weather, whether we want to or not."
+ "Lucious slushies, luscious slushies, luscious slushies, luscious slushies."
+ "Essex's niece's needs exceed Essex's nephew's needs."

PRACTICE OR PERFORMANCE?

Unless you're leading a meeting about the importance of onomatopoeia, warming up is obviously a practice exercise. In any discipline, warming up happens before. So, too, with communicating.

PRO TIP

I've hinted at this already in my instructions for the tongue twisters, but now I'll say it explicitly: Go far with the warm-ups. If they don't feel like you're "stretching," like you're exploring the full range of your communication instrument, the activity is not giving you as much benefit as it could. Do not misinterpret this advice and injure yourself! I'm not talking about pushing your body beyond what it can do. I mean push more from an intentionality standpoint. See how much you can move your mouth when you do the tongue twisters, for example.

WHAT ABOUT VIRTUAL?

Virtual communication is a boon to these activities because one frequent excuse is removed: "I don't have anywhere to warm up or to do the exercises beforehand." Whereas ducking down the hall, finding an available bathroom, and doing physical warm-ups silently in a cramped bathroom stall is sometimes necessary at work to find a bit of private space, remote work has given everyone the possibility to warm up with complete abandon and then "enter" the workplace by logging in to a virtual meeting.

So when you are working from home, warm up early and often!

CHAPTER 17

NAVIGATING NERVES

How to Learn to Love Anxiety (and Stop Worrying)

G reetings! My name is Michael Chad Hoeppner, and I'm going to help you communicate better when it counts.

For those of you who have read all the preceding chapters—no, I am not suffering from amnesia; I haven't forgotten that we've already spent hundreds of pages together. But I know some of you are meeting me in this chapter for the very first time—because you immediately flipped to this point the moment you procured the book. Why? Many of you are frustrated—perhaps even at your wits' end—about the maddening, deranging experience of constantly battling nerves in important situations.

Why bury this chapter so near the end, then? Why not address this widespread pain point first so we can get it out of the way?

Because even though nerves may be your biggest pain point, they are not the most important point. And the bigger a deal we make about nerves, often the worse they get. So I have relegated them to Chapter 17. Deal with it, Nerves! You got outranked by Stance. You could probably handle being after Brevity or Eye Contact...but Stance? How dare I not treat you with the terrified reverence to which you're accustomed!

Since this is only the seventeenth-most important chapter in the book, for those of you who have started here, please go back to the beginning and read from page 1. Go ahead, please.

(I'm waiting.)

(I'm still waiting. . . .)

Weird. You're continuing in this chapter even though the author—who has spent no small amount of time fashioning and refashioning each of these words in this precise order—has requested that you do so.

Why are you rebelling?

I know why: even with the explicit instruction not to do so, the pull and promise of having the antidote to severe nerves is too tempting to follow any instruction besides "Get the antidote!"

And yet . . . I'm going to make you wait multiple paragraphs *more* before you get the antidote.

AGONY!

How could I be so cruel? How could I prattle on at the beginning of this chapter for almost five hundred words just talking about the subject—and now talking about talking about the subject—when I could just cut to the chase and give you the damn antidote?!

Because.

Because even regarding the subject itself, I want to provoke you to interrogate your thinking about "nerves."

Are your nerves really the villain they seem?

Or could it be that your judgment and critique of your nerves are the actual villains?

Consider two concepts: distance and distraction. The goal I suggest you embrace is not "to make your nerves go away." You and your nerves do not need to be mortal enemies, forever locked in a battle to the death. In that relationship you try to overcome, conquer, suppress, combat, fight, or defeat your nerves. You might win one skirmish with them, but inevitably they resurface and defeat you, thereby shaking your faith in your own abilities even further as you layer shame and self-loathing on top of your already wicked self-judgment about your supposed failure in a communication situation (I say "supposed" only because your performance may not have been as bad as you think!).

Your shame and self-loathing probably sound something like this: "I'm such a fool! I thought I was better! I thought I had a tool! But I'm a naive, weak sucker. I should never have thought that I was free. I choke; I always choke. I'm doomed to perpetually choke, and I shouldn't have the temerity to hope not to choke; I should just crawl into my cave of self-criticism and never come out (and certainly never again put myself in a high-consequence communication situation!) because I know what will happen, so I should just spare the world from myself."

I'm laying it on a bit thick (or maybe not, for some of you). If that inner monologue rings a bell—welcome! You're at home. Come on out of your shame cave and wrap yourself in the pages of this chapter.

What getting *distance* from your nerves means is this. Imagine you're on a street somewhere with a violently angry bully; they're screaming insults, epithets, profanity. You—being the streetwise imaginary city dweller that you are—walk deliberately and calmly away from them. You can still hear their ranting from the other side of the street, but as you continue navigating the city, their voice slowly fades and you return to the *distraction* of your cell phone, attending to the thousands of things on your to-do list.

You probably think you know where I'm going with this: That screaming bully is your nerves. But, no—you're wrong. That screaming bully is you! That screaming bully is your narrative of impossible instructions (just relax!), catastrophic pronouncements (you always choke!), and belittling insults (you're a fraud!) that you berate yourself with while you're trying to communicate-when-nervous. That screaming, out-of-control bully is you verbally assaulting yourself about your nerves. That is you "battling" your nerves.

In the street metaphor, you would of course be insane to walk up to that bully and start a fight. That bully is just hoping that someone will engage with them so they can shout them down and instigate the confrontation they're oh-so eager to have. In the street, you would simply get distance from the bully. In navigating your nerves, the mission is the same: just get distance from the yelling. You'll probably still hear it, but the farther away you get (distance) and the more engrossed in your cell phone (distraction), the less you'll notice it.

That's our goal: distance and distraction. And they reinforce each other. The more fully absorbed you can get in something else (distraction), the faster that yelling bully will fade away (distance).

Not a city dweller? Let's consider a different metaphor, and this time let's give your actual nerves—not just the reaction to and judgment about them—an identity too. Imagine you're an elementary school student, and you have brought a pet (a sweet little dog, perhaps) for show-and-tell. You're in the schoolyard at recess before show-and-tell, and your pet—though you love it dearly—is a mess. It is hyper, jumping everywhere, trembling because it is surrounded by a whole bunch of strangers. Maybe it even peed somewhere it shouldn't have out of sheer terror. A schoolyard bully sees an opening and begins to ridicule you mercilessly. The ineffective response is this: Take the bait and get sucked into the bully's goading. Instead, take the dog and go run a lap. Soon the other kids might even join you as the dog—now occupied with the fun activity of running—transforms from terrified to joyous and playfully tries to grab the leash as it runs.

The dog is your nerves. The bully is your inner tyrannical, mean-spirited critic. If you get sucked into battling the bully, the bully is thrilled to have a co-combatant, and you just get more and more agitated and upset. Meanwhile, the dog probably gets even more freaked out. If, on the other hand, you run the dog, the bully's voice gets physically and psychically farther away, the dog has an outlet for its energy, and you feel better as you run—relieved, relaxed, and maybe even joyous.

So, if you struggle with nerves, let me offer a powerful mindset shift: *stop trying to stop them.*

Remember the lessons from this book's early chapters: (1) thought suppression is impossible; (2) General Don't feedback like "Don't be nervous, just be yourself" is worthless; and (3) you don't need to feel confident in order to project confidence. I remind you of those lessons because people typically go about addressing nerves in a completely counterproductive manner—they try to make the nerves go away.

For those of you familiar with meditation, this concept will resonate. Meditators are encouraged to simply notice their thoughts rather than prevent or stop them, to observe them as passing clouds that drift into their consciousness and then drift away.

Performers are trained to go a step further. Not only are they coached to notice rather than stop their nerves—just like athletes perfecting complex moves—performers develop positive muscle memory that they can rely on even when nervous. Every drill you just learned in this book has that same purpose.

So, this day, this hour, this moment, I want you to end your lifetime journey of searching for a way to stop being nervous. It's not your job to not be nervous. Your job is simply to communicate capably in different situations. If you're nervous in those situations, fine. If you're not, fine.

That's easier said than done, of course. So let's stop just saying and get to some doing. I want you to try an activity that examines how arbitrary our nervous reactions can be.

What do I mean by arbitrary? With nerves, many, many people identify specific scenarios as the cause or culprit; yet an identical scenario with just one factor changed isn't even challenging. For some, standing up and giving a speech is terrifying, but if they can be seated, they're fine. Or if they're talking to a faceless mass in a remote webinar, they're paralyzed with nerves, but in a room with a live audience, they're fine. Or maybe if they must stick to a precise script, they're earth-rattlingly anxious, but if they can speak using bullet points, they're fine.

The most obvious boundary where we can begin to dissect this phenomenon is "number of people in the audience." I often make clients commit to a certain threshold number at which point they enter Nervous Land to force them to acknowledge how arbitrary their distinction actually is. Is the boundary between four and five audience members the point at which "just talking" shifts to "public speaking"? Is it between nine and ten? You will soon see that many, many of the distinctions that are supposedly the cause of your nerves are absurdly arbitrary—almost random—maybe even silly.

Consider the following pairings. Please go through each row, and circle which of the two situations makes you more nervous. If neither makes you nervous (or both make you equally nervous), you can ignore that row.

In person	Remote
Using notes	Being unscripted
Presenting with a deck	Speaking without slides
Word-for-word speech	Outline with bullet points
Formal presentation	Free-form discussion
Random audience	Colleagues and friends
Standing	Sitting
Stationary podium	Open stage
No audience interaction	Q&A

I have tried to pack this book chock-full of profound and important questions. But now—regarding all the distinctions you just made—I'm going to ask you one of the only worthless questions in this entire book.

Here it is: *Why?*

Why do you feel nervous in those situations and cool as a cucumber in others?

My answer is the answer I invite you to adopt also:

Who cares?!

I have no idea why that one arbitrary distinction makes you nervous and why its opposite doesn't. You will probably want to cling to some highly rational explanation: "Well, I once was kidnapped by a Power-Point designer and ever since I've been traumatized by slides."

If you want to interrogate that distinction further, here's another provocative question: What about that one time when that specific situation *didn't* make you nervous? You know. That one time when you were surprisingly calm in the situation that always makes you terrified?

C'mon. Be honest with yourself. You don't know why!

Who. Cares?

If you really want to plumb the depths of your soul and discover an absolute why in a lengthy and rewarding therapeutic process, be my guest.

But I would encourage you not to hold out hope for nailing down the why. You'll probably learn a lot, but you still may not find a final why.

Because there might not be a why.

(Minds blown.)

Maybe consider accepting that you "just get nervous" in those situations. That might feel like relief.

Regardless of whether you accept and embrace this, here's the most amazing, liberating, thrilling news of all: you don't have to know why you have nerves in those situations to get better at navigating them.

So, let's leave the realm of the why and consider the how. How are you going to get better at navigating nerves? Like a much-hyped self-help book that touts the secret to enlightenment, self-actualization, or instant wealth, this book has a secret. *Shhhhhhhh.* But unlike other snake oil sales devices, this secret works wonders, and works permanently. But it is hard work and takes time and diligence.

Here it is: The thing that will allow you to navigate your nerves is finding concrete, actionable, and useful things to focus on in place of obsessing about them—essentially, gaining distance via useful distraction. What kind of things? For starters, you can begin with all the stuff you read and learned in Chapters 1 through 16! All those exercises and tools are far more useful places to put your attention than "Don't Be Nervous."

If it's a tool from this or any of the previous chapters, here's what you're looking for: you have to learn to focus on something that is physical, unmistakable, and integrated.

Those are three big adjectives. What the heck do they mean?

1. You must find a physical focus; it can't just be a thought.
2. You must find an unmistakable focus; you must be able to accurately diagnose whether you did—or did not—do it.
3. You must find an integrated focus; it must be integrated into the act of communicating and therefore aligned with your purpose rather than unrelated or even oppositional.

Never fear—I will explain how each of these work as we go.

What *do* you *do* with this point of focus once you have found it? You must *do* it and *do* it relentlessly. This will allow you to use your squirrelly, misbehaving brain against itself.

Your brain—contrary to what you might think—is not great at multitasking. In fact, multitasking is an illusion. It's really task switching. We think we're multitasking; we're actually just switching between tasks very quickly and chronically. Each shift exacts a cognitive toll (that is, it uses a bunch of energy and concentration). If you've paid attention to recent research about digital notifications, our under-siege attention spans, or the effect newsfeed doomscrolling has on your brain, none of this is a surprise to you.

Great news! You can exploit your brain's inability to multitask. When you find something more immediate and actionable than your nerves and then continually focus on it, your nerves will fade and fade and fade and fade. . . .

As I introduced earlier, this is what performers are trained to do. (And now you are too!) They don't vilify their nerves; they simply make another point of concentration more important.

Let me share an example. My wife is an incredible, world-class singer. Yet the first time she sang at Carnegie Hall, she was so nervous her knees were literally knocking, bouncing rapidly like a rock climber with "type-writer leg" at the end of a grueling pitch. As she stood in the wings waiting to take the stage, she reminded herself to walk to the mic and then put every ounce of her focus on using her lips to fully enunciate her final voiced consonants (technical speak for the ends of words). Sounds deadly simple, doesn't it? Yes. That's the point.

And it might surprise you to know that accurate, percussive enunciation isn't even a struggle for her! Rather, it's easy. In that moment of absolute terror, it was the quickest, easiest thing to focus on. She focused on enunciating every word as clearly as possible (instead of fixating on the nightmare scenario of forgetting the lyrics of a song). As she did, she was able to tap into the Virtuous Cycle of Good Communication we examined in Chapter 4, and—in a matter of a few musical bars—she was able to breathe, look in her concertgoers' eyes, and actually enjoy a moment of performance she had worked her entire life to earn.

That's not to impress you about her or her musicianship; it is rather to impress you about her approach.

You're likely not singing at Carnegie Hall. But the same tools can help you sing the music of your professional communication.

I'll share another example. I have tried to use a very accessible tone in writing this book. I want you to feel (because it's the truth!) that I am in your corner and can relate to your victories and struggles. But you might also think I'm not relatable—"That dude coaches presidential candidates and gives presentations around the world. I'm sure he never gets nervous."

Well, to put that hypothesis to rest, I'll share a ridiculous, absurd situation in which I felt outlandishly nervous: speaking at a local school board meeting. That's right. Speaking to a viewing audience of *zero* (trust me, no one was attending this particular school board meeting), I felt my heart rate skyrocket and the butterflies in my stomach flutter like streamers in a hurricane. But here's the biggest difference about where I currently am as a speaker and where you likely are: I never asked myself why I was having that reaction, nor did I try to make it go away. Why was I nervous to speak at the school board meeting? I have no idea. And truthfully—who cares?

All I focused on in that moment was posture. That's it. From a lifetime of speaking in situations that matter, I have built the muscle memory to use more of myself (not less) when nervous, and so I focused on my head floating toward the ceiling, opened my mouth, and spoke.

And you can do the same thing.

What specific focus should *you* choose?

Let's return to the criteria I introduced earlier.

- You must find a physical focus. It can't just be a thought.
  * Why must it be physical? As you know well at this point in the book (or as you're learning now if this is your first chapter), when it comes to speaking, your body is more reliable than your brain. So identify a physical practice rather than a mental one.
- You must find an unmistakable focus; you must be able to accurately diagnose whether you did—or did not—do it.
  * Why must the focus be unmistakable? You need to be able to distinguish when you are doing the behavior.

Importantly, that is not the same thing as qualitatively evaluating your performance, for example, "I was 'good'" or "I was 'bad.'" I don't care about subjective impressions of good or bad. I care about something far simpler and more accurate. For example: Did your lips move sufficiently when you made *p*, *b*, *w*, and *m* sounds, or did they not?

- You must find an integrated focus; it must be integrated into the act of communicating and therefore aligned with your purpose rather than unrelated or even oppositional.
  * Why must you find an integrated focus? It needs to be in service of your communication rather than merely a competing, alternative subject.

To put those criteria into stark relief, let's consider a popular—even famous—strategy that sounds like it fulfills the need for another focus: imagining your audience in their underwear. We've all heard this. Purportedly, it's an imperceptible, sly way to unlock better performance. The speaker has an irreverent secret that allows them to see their audience as a sea of emperors with no clothes, robbing the audience of its threat and status.

The problem? For most people, it doesn't work. Let's examine why.

- Is it physical? No. It's a mental activity.
- Is it unmistakable? Probably not. If you accept that we are bad at multitasking, it stands to reason it will be very hard to think about both naked people and the words you should say at the same time.
- Is it integrated into the act of communicating? No! This is the measurement it fails the most. It is essentially a different topic, totally unrelated to the act of turning air into words, and in fact practically a non sequitur.

FIRST, FIND YOUR FOCUS

If you're not going to use the ol' Try to Picture Them in Their Underwear technique, what should you choose as your point of focus?

At this point in the book, you may have already chosen it! (Or rather, it may have chosen you.) If in the first sixteen chapters you have discovered a specific tool that absorbs your concentration, shifts a behavior, and improves your overall performance, that may be it. Here are just some examples:

+ Grounding your feet on the floor (stance via book standing, the shoe exercise, or "nailing" your feet to the floor)
+ Pausing intentionally at the end of thoughts (pausing via Lego block exercise or variations thereof)
+ Using freer, more expressive gestures (gestures via Silent Storytelling)
+ Eliciting specific responses and reactions from your audience (audience focus via ball throwing)
+ Using more variety and energy in your voice (Five Ps of Vocal Variety, via Silent Storytelling, Play Your Horn Hand, Lego blocks for variety, etc.)
+ Feeling your back side ribs expanding with air when you breathe (breathing via balloon exercise and Play Your Horn Hand)
+ Using your lips and tongue as precisely as possible to ensure your diction is exact (enunciation via cork/impediment exercise)

You don't necessarily need to choose something that is challenging for you. It can be something you're good at. If you'll recall my wife's story about singing at Carnegie Hall, she didn't choose enunciation because she knew hers was sloppy or poor; she chose enunciation because it was actually quite easy for her to execute. The essential measurement here is not level of difficulty but level of commitment. You must commit 100 percent.

CHAPTER 17
NAVIGATING NERVES

And if you choose one focus and then you find a better one later, great! There is no final exam in this book. You're not going to be asked to pass the bar. So choose the best, most-likely-to-succeed tool for you, and recognize you might find even better ones as you experiment.

In fact, it's quite likely as you get better and better at this (which you will), your focus will naturally shift. You will begin to unlock the Virtuous Cycle of Good Communication and, for example, enunciation will lead to breath and breath to posture and posture to vocal variety and so on and so on. You may grow to enjoy, even, how your focus grows and shifts over time.

DIP YOUR TOES IN THE WATER

Once you have found what your focus is, now you must practice it—a lot. To start that, I recommend you begin by wading into the shallow end first. This means embracing what I call low-consequence opportunities. Choose scenarios in which you have no or almost no risk. Use those as your practice arena. Become excellent at remaining laser focused on your skill in those situations. Then broaden. Next choose some situations that are slightly higher stakes. Keep going with that process, slowly but surely, as you increase the difficulty level of your scenarios.

If you have chosen something that is inappropriate to practice in public situations (you can't talk with a cork in your mouth during meetings), adjust the focus so it is imperceptible. With the cork example, focus solely on your enunciation, and do it so deliberately that you can feel the corners of your mouth moving and working as decisively as when they have a frustratingly large impediment (the cork) in their way. As an example, I coach the leader of a famous university. The Lego drill was transformative for him. So we practiced it enough that he was able to shift it to an imperceptible activity. He built the muscle memory to find a tiny moment of physical stillness at the end of each thought. To commit to this 100 percent, when on video calls—and when nervous or anxious—he places his hand on his desk, subtly and imperceptibly. This muscle-memory skill has allowed him to pause and consider what he wants to say next, even in fraught situations.

LET YOURSELF OFF THE HOOK

Once you have found your focus, practiced it in low-consequence situations, and built some muscle memory, you're ready to give it a test drive in higher-stakes situations. Here I recommend being as inventive as possible and finding an on-ramp to start from a position of comfort. Let me explain what I mean.

It is very rare that you have absolute restriction on what you can and cannot do as a speaker. Remember all those arbitrary distinctions you circled at the beginning of this chapter? When speaking, give yourself a helping hand—if possible, start in the mode that is easier for you and then shift to what is more challenging. I'll give you some examples.

- If a formal script is difficult for you, start by freelancing a bit, and then segue into your formal remarks. Perhaps even tell your audience, with full transparency, that you now "want to read some prepared remarks because it's so essential I don't leave any of this out." Is there a law that you can't tell people you're reading from a script? No! Might that statement liberate you from having to pretend that you're not reading? Yes!

- If speaking free-form is challenging, mark up your notes in three places and give yourself a precise task for those instances: Maybe one is "share anecdote," another is "offer to answer any questions," and the third is "walk through the numbers." Might bracketing where you need to speak in a free-form manner help you feel some security? Yes!

- If talking into a video camera is nerve-racking, tell the person running the camera that you want to do two full run-throughs of what you're going to say, and they should just let the camera keep recording throughout. As soon as you finish the first, just keep going and do a second "take" immediately. Might having the first, slightly stiffer version of your content out of the way make the second one that follows looser? Yes!

+ If talking to a large audience is scary, begin by talking to one person. As you're walking to the front of the room, tap someone on their shoulder, shake their hand, and say something extremely positive to them: "Good to see you!" or "Glad you could make it" or "Right at the front—I like it!" Might giving your body a chance to say some words out loud to one person before addressing many give you a baby step into your remarks? Yes!

+ If standing is scary, find a way to begin seated and then gravitate to standing. You can tell your audience you're doing so. "In a moment I'll stand up and walk us through some material on the large screen, but I'd like to begin just with a discussion to find out more about what's on your minds." Might giving your body a few minutes to present while seated ease the transition to standing? Yes!

+ If "presenting" makes you nervous, but "discussing" doesn't, begin your presentation with questions to the audience. Again, you can tell them you're doing so. "I'd like to make today as applicable to you as possible, so I want to start off with a couple questions." And then ask your audience some questions. Once you're in the flow of the Q&A, segue into your content. Might giving yourself the reminder that all presentations are ultimately a response to a question help you present conversationally? Yes!

+ If copresenting helps you feel more secure, enlist a copresenter or demonstrator/volunteer at the beginning. Then challenge yourself to have that volunteer take up less and less of the initial time at the beginning of your presentation and eventually shift to solo presenting. Might having a partner in crime de-escalate your perception of pressure? Yes!

These are all examples of how to do something you probably haven't done to this point: Be nice to yourself. No one says you must execute the very-highest-level-of-difficulty act. So don't—yet. Find your focus, practice it a ton, slowly transition to higher-stakes opportunities, and build on-ramps for yourself that allow you to start with something you're more comfortable with and then shift to what's less comfortable once you're cookin'.

We're almost to the end of this chapter. You may be surprised by a few things we haven't covered, like visualization, breathing exercises, and/or drugs.

Many people: (1) visualize their performance in advance; (2) use box breathing, 1:3:2 performance breathing, or some other type of intentional breathing to center themselves; and/or (3) rely on blood pressure medications to medically manage their heart rate before presenting.

If visualizing, meditative breathing, or beta-blockers are tools you use and realize benefit from, far be it from me to remove effective tools. I don't make those tactics a focus of my coaching practice because I don't see them deliver the level of utility that everything else I have just offered in this chapter does. Hence, my approach.

Beta-blockers, as an example, are medications some people use to alter their blood pressure before presenting. The net result is they get less of the racing-heart symptoms that often frustrate them in high-stakes situations. Sounds like a miracle cure, right? Consider this though: Many actors who use beta-blockers during a period of their career for important auditions or performances drift away from using them long-term because the medication can also dull some of the quicksilver moments that heightened attention—and, yes, nerves—unlock. So the electricity of their performance might dim.

I make no claims, recommendations, or diagnoses about anything pharmacological—I have no qualifications to! I only mention beta-blockers because you may have encountered or will encounter them in discussions about nerves. If you did use, are using, or will use medication to navigate nerves, I neither suggest you do or do not use them. I am not a doctor (nor did I ever play one on TV), so I will sidestep the subject matter entirely.

I will examine each of the other tactics in case you want to try them. Every word in this book is intended to help you find a level of liberation and freedom with communicating and a release valve from perfectionism and self-critique. Explore these tools, too, if you like.

Please keep in mind that the following activities are preparatory activities. They are things you do before you do the thing. This is part of the reason why I recommend them as optional and not mandatory. For some people, they're helpful preparation; for others, they're not. For everyone, they aren't in-the-moment adjustments. And the ultimate test of whatever nerves strategy you employ is this: Can you do it while you're communicating when nervous? That test is why I recommend the approach that I do in this chapter. So the mandatory, primary lesson from this chapter is *finding, practicing, and mastering your physical, unmistakable, and integrated focus.* The optional ones are in these next few paragraphs.

- First, just as we did moments ago, you can rely on the warm-ups in the previous chapter—full-body movement, tongue twisters, yawns, etc.—to both wake up and relax your body physically before communicating.
- Second, you can do a series of tense-and-release activities. They're as simple as they sound: Tense all your muscles as much as possible, and then release them. Tense for three seconds, then release. Do that three times. Then do it for six seconds, also three times. You can experiment with the length of time that feels ideal to you.
- Third, you can explore box breathing and 1:3:2 performance breath. Box breathing is simply using equal time in four stages of the breath cycle: inhale, hold, exhale, hold. For example, you can inhale for a count of three; hold for a count of three; exhale for a count of three; and hold for a count of three. You can then tinker with the length of time but keep it identical for each of the four stages.

  1:3:2 breathing is similar, but this technique uses unequal amounts of time in three stages of the breath cycle: one count of breathing in; three counts of holding the breath; and two counts of breathing out. To unleash the benefit of this drill, keep in mind the following technical requirements. First, breathe in as much as you can in the first stage. That means the first round of doing this will feature a very quick and expansive first breath; get as much air into your body as possible in one count. The second phase is straightforward:

hold your breath. In the third phase, focus on evacuating all your air in the time allowed, and to help you do that, exhale on a sustained *s* sound.

Next, double and then triple the length of time in each stage. So, the time allocations become 2:6:4 and then 3:9:6.

Unlike in other sections, I'm not going to try to motivate you to do the techniques and exercises in this chapter or the full approach of finding, practicing, and mastering your physical, unmistakable, integrated focus or the warm-up and breathing activities just outlined. I'm guessing that if navigating nerves is a challenge for you, you have all the motivation you need to implement and experiment with these tools ASAP, without any nudging! They are to be practiced and performed; they apply when you are live and when virtual.

This means we can move on to an essential related topic, which is the source of a lot of speakers' nerves in the first place: the fear of "What If I Make a Mistake?"

And that's the topic of our final skill-building chapter.

CHAPTER 18

RECOVERING FROM MISTAKES

How to Embrace Transparency (and Avoid Hiding)

One of the core sources of nerves for people is, to quote Franklin Delano Roosevelt, fear itself. People are terrorized by the thought "What if I mess up?" The fear of messing up often makes the likelihood of messing up higher because it amps communicators' nerves so much that it makes it harder for them to think of the words they're striving to say. How can you disarm the mistakes yet to come? Think of all the "mistakes" we make when speaking: verbal stumbles; misapplied metaphors; errors or typos on a presentation slide; outdated facts or statistics; incorrect information. We all say lots and lots of wrong, poorly executed, or unintended stuff.

I suggest for all these situations and more that you unlock the power of a tool you already use but forget when you become self-focused: transparency. Transparency can mean a lot of different things in different situations, but for our purposes I mean acknowledging, naming, and owning what's happening in a given moment in fully transparent language. In the next few paragraphs, I would like to convince you of the following mantra: "A Mistake Is Not a Mistake."

When humans are tremendously other-focused, they live this mantra without even thinking about it. If your best friend were going through a crisis and you mistakenly gave them the wrong contact information for a lawyer, would you feel any awkwardness about correcting it? No! If you were helping a lost tourist and you mistakenly gave them the wrong street name, would you feel any awkwardness about correcting it? No! Yet when "presenting," people feel obligated to be entirely mistake free. And that rigid focus on being flawless derails them. The goal I invite you to embrace is flexibility, not flawlessness.

What does this look like in practice? I once coached a gentleman from Germany who speaks five languages. At times, his English was difficult to understand. He was stuck in a vicious cycle in which he would make a mistake in grammar or pronunciation and then try to hide that mistake with two unhelpful behaviors. First, he would physically contract—literally try to shrink. This was his attempt to prevent people from noticing him. Second, he would talk faster. This was his attempt to prevent people from noticing his mistake.

Do you think either attempt worked?

No. Those two behaviors made his mistakes more noticeable, not less. So instead of trying to hide or disguise his mistakes, I coached him to use transparency unabashedly by creating and integrating transparency phrases. I coached him to say things like the following when he made a pronunciation "mistake": "Pardon me—I speak five languages. Sometimes English pronunciation is difficult. How do you pronounce that word?"

By employing that tool, he accomplished three things in one fell swoop. First, he subtly but unmistakably educated his audience about his multilingual abilities ("He speaks five languages!"). Second, he reflected the energy of the interaction back to his audience. We all want to feel intelligent and capable of pronouncing words. So when his audience was given the opportunity to display intelligence and accurate pronunciation, they felt valuable. And third, he relieved himself of any obligation to hide. His relief was so profound that very soon he discovered he didn't even need the transparency phrase. Why? Because his big and powerful brain—now relieved of the burden of avoiding every mistake in the future and camouflaging every one in the past—was liberated to actually think about what he wanted to say in the first place! He had a tool. And because of that tool, he actually thought of words more accurately and speedily. His mistakes didn't happen as frequently.

Let's consider another example—a universal one that's relevant regardless of the number of languages you speak. If you're drawing on a flip chart in front of a room and the marker doesn't work, is it better to hide the marker behind your back and pretend you weren't writing, or is it better to say, "This marker doesn't work, I'll try another one"? If you pick up a second marker and it doesn't work either, is it better to hide the marker behind your back and pretend you weren't writing, or is it better to say, "This marker doesn't work either. Apparently, we need a new marker budget"? (You can probably surmise my answer from my leading questions.)

The marker is a piece of technology. It has a filament, the filament is soaked in ink, and when you press the filament to a piece of paper, the ink gets expelled. It's a fairly primitive piece of technology, but a piece of technology nonetheless. PowerPoint is also technology—some might say equally as primitive as the marker. In that hypothetical moment, you were failed by technology. Who else has ever been failed by technology at some point in their life? Any person you will ever speak to in any audience anywhere.

When you are transparent, you do two powerful things. One, you let your audience know that you are alive in the present moment—no small feat in our modern smart-device-riddled world! And, two, you engage your audience's empathy. And if you have engaged an audience's empathy, as a presenter you are halfway home.

To get very specific, I'd like to teach you the Three Fs of Transparency. You're probably familiar with three other Fs that pervade mistake moments in presentation situations (and that I mentioned briefly in Chapter 9): fight, flight, or freeze. Those, of course, are the three typical crisis responses humans resort to when under threat. Those tactics might work well for fleeing a saber-toothed tiger; they are less effective when behind a podium. So I invite you to replace those three Fs with these: Fake it, Fix it, and Feature it. Those are the Three Fs of Transparency.

You might be wondering how on earth the first F can be Fake it, given that I've just spent two pages proving to you that you don't have to Fake it when you make mistakes. I'm not suggesting that every time you make any type of mistake or error you must bring it to your audience's attention. If no one will notice, if you can proceed without it throwing you off—Fake it! But if the "mistake" is threatening to undermine you in the least—if you are going to spend the next ten minutes obsessing about your "mistake" while simultaneously trying to continue speaking—you have two great options.

One, you can Fix it. That might sound something like "The Power-Point clicker isn't working at the moment, so I'll just sit with my laptop and advance the slides manually." Or you can Feature it, which means that you position the moment as a positive thing. That might sound something like "The PowerPoint clicker isn't working, which is actually a great reminder to talk about updating our infrastructure and technology."

Now you get to draft your own transparency phrase, just as I coached the German gentleman to do. Please write down a statement that you could use to course correct when (not if) you make a "mistake." That might be something like any of the following:

LET ME GO BACK FOR A MOMENT. . . .
LET ME CLARIFY THAT. . . .
HERE'S A BETTER WAY TO PUT IT. . . .
ACTUALLY, WHAT I MEAN IS . . .
LET'S START AGAIN. . . .
TAKING A STEP BACK . . .
ON SECOND THOUGHT . . .

WRITE YOURS HERE:

_____

NOW WRITE ANOTHER TWO (BECAUSE LIFE HAS PLENTY
OF MISTAKES IN STORE FOR YOU):

_____

_____

CHAPTER 18
RECOVERING FROM MISTAKES

* * *

Hopefully, just the act of choosing a phrase and writing it down feels delicious and liberating, as you envision how using this phrase like a Get Out of Jail Free card might transform your performance as well as your perception of pressure. But writing it down is just the beginning. It's time to make some visual aids.

You wrote three transparency phrases; following, you'll see six others. In a second you can turn the page and check them out, but first let me explain what they are. They look roughly like playing cards. I use these cards with my clients to help desensitize them to mistakes. If you feel emboldened to use this book like the how-to manual that it is, cut them out! In a moment, take the pages, and tear or cut along the dotted lines to give yourself six cards with six different transparency phrases. If you don't want to further deface your already tatter-torn copy of *Don't Say Um*, you can also just write those phrases on sticky notes or scraps of paper. Or you can get your own set. These six cards are one set in a larger card game tool we designed for our clients called Conversation. If you want to get the full game—or just the six transparency cards—you can do so at dontsayum.com.

Note that none of the cards features the words *I'm sorry*. An apology is for when you have done something wrong. Mistakes often simply require a correction, not an apology.

Perhaps just glancing at those cards (or the sticky notes you scrawled) has already inspired you to navigate challenges, mishaps, and course corrections unabashedly.

But you know me: at this point, we have to make this kinesthetic so your body remembers it, not just your brain.

What comes next requires balance and dexterity. If I were coaching you in person, I would have you talk while standing on one leg. Then I would repeatedly and randomly push you (ever so gently) so that you would have to put your elevated foot back on the floor to avoid falling over. As you placed your foot down to keep your balance, I would ask you to say the mantra, "A Mistake Is Not a Mistake." Then you would lift your foot again to reassume a one-legged stance and continue speaking.

GK ♥transparency
cards

♥transparency

let me
clarify that...

♥transparency

in other
words...

♥transparency

oh! I can't
believe I
forgot, I also
want to say...

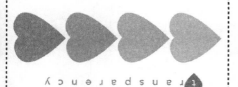

♥transparency

let me
go back a
moment...

GK transparency cards

♥ transparency

that's not
what I meant,
what I meant
was...

transparency

COPYRIGHT GK TRAINING

♥ transparency

what does
that mean?

transparency

COPYRIGHT GK TRAINING

Then we would go further, and instead of saying the A Mistake Is Not a Mistake mantra, I would require you to say the six specific transparency phrases on the cards in random order as I pushed you over repeatedly. I created this exercise for my clients because it physicalizes the ostensibly perilous moment of making a mistake: "Oh no! I'm off balance! I'm about to fall/fail!" But in the instant of recovery that follows—when the speaker has both feet on the ground—they get the relief of safety. Their body gets the experience that not only is a mistake not a crisis—it's not even a mistake.

In essence, it's desensitization training. I desensitize my clients to the act of making a "mistake."

I used this exercise once with a senior partner at a venerable financial firm. This gentleman fit all the cliché stereotypes of the Wall Street Master of the Universe archetype. Yet this gentleman got choked up in this activity and was moved to tears. I gave him a moment to live through the experience. Then I asked him gently about his reaction. "I wasn't crying because I was scared or upset," he said. "For the first time, I just felt self-forgiveness." He forgave himself for the "mistakes"; he gave himself license to be imperfect.

Now: Let's manage expectations for a moment. This drill may not be a cathartic life-changer for you. Let's not saddle it with undoing years of perfectionism. But . . . for those perfectionists out there, don't be shocked if this modest exercise creates some major epiphanies.

Because I'm not sharing the same space with you, we must adjust the drill so that even without my arbitrarily timed shoves we can create an essential element: randomness. We must create a situation in which you are not in control of when you have to adapt or course correct because, although you can certainly predict that mistakes will happen, you rarely can predict *when*. To create that random, unpredictable timing, we're going to enlist the help of an unlikely partner: water. You will need two things—a working sink you can stand near and a tiny container that can be filled with water. I do mean tiny. A thimble, bottle cap, contact lens case, or something similar will do the trick. I'll explain the drill, and then you can navigate to a sink and try it.

When you are ready to begin the exercise, place the container under the faucet in a stable position so it can fill with water without tipping.

Once the container is positioned, turn the faucet on at a miniscule drip so that the container gradually fills with water. Begin speaking on professional content and use something extensive enough that you can speak for five to ten minutes. You will see the gradual drip-drip-drip of water fill up the container; at some point, the surface tension is no longer sufficient to contain the water, and some portion of it will spill over. That is the moment you are watching for because that is your cue to use a transparency phrase.

For the first incarnation of the drill, when those spillover moments happen, I want you to: (1) say "A Mistake Is Not a Mistake" out loud; (2) pour out the water in the container and return it to position; and (3) continue speaking from wherever you left off (or shift to a different portion of your content). Do the exercise long enough that you have six to eight instances of saying that mantra.

The next version incorporates the cards. When doing the drill, you'll spread them out face side up next to the sink so that you can see the text of each card. Do the drill again, but this time instead of saying the Mistake Is Not a Mistake mantra when the spillover moment happens, choose one of the six cards and say whatever phrase is on that card. Then do the same steps as before: empty the water, reposition the cup, and continue speaking. Do this series until you have used all six cards (each card can be used only once).

Then you'll be ready for the last version. It's the same exercise, but with an added level of difficulty because you'll be saying a randomly chosen transparency phrase. In this version, shuffle the six cards and place them face down near the sink. Do the water droplet activity again, but this time at each spillover moment draw a card from the top of the pile and say whatever transparency phrase you have just randomly selected. Here it is step-by-step one final time: (1) talk, and when the spillover happens, pick up the top card and say its phrase; (2) empty the container and return it to its place; and (3) keep talking.

Ready to try? I thought so! Go find a container and sink and try each of the versions of this activity. I'll see you back here shortly....

*　*　*

What did you discover? If you're like many of the people around the world to whom I've taught this exercise, as you got accustomed to the drill, not only were you able to continue speaking, but also your speaking may have improved through the arc of the exercise! Embracing the inevitable bumps and bruises that come along may have freed you up to use more vocal variety, more gestural freedom, more enunciation, more, more, more.

I like the water version of this activity because the sensory experience makes it very memorable, but there are other tools. If you have an old-fashioned handheld kitchen timer, you can use that. Whenever the timer rings, instead of adjusting the flow of the sink, quickly and randomly turn the dial somewhere in the one- to three-minute range. Or use the timer app on your smartphone. Select the timer function, set it to forty-five seconds to start. Then each time you say the mantra or use a card, reset the time—quickly and sloppily spin the number of seconds so that you're adapting to different intervals of time. (You can also get the minutes column involved, but you will get more payoff from this drill by doing many course corrections and adjustments, so condensed intervals are preferred.)

PRACTICE OR PERFORMANCE?

This drill is both a practice and a performance one. The practice version utilizes the cards and some device to create randomness. But the performance one is simply this: Use transparency to navigate the inevitable mistakes that inhabit all our communication lives. As you do this, you will begin to see these principles everywhere. And you may even want to institute them beyond your communication. After all, navigating mistakes with grace and transparency isn't just good in communication; it's good in life. And it's not just good for your audience; it's good for you, as our titan of Wall Street realized.

WHAT ABOUT VIRTUAL?

Using transparency when communicating virtually is even more powerful. Why? Because it can not only help you navigate mistakes but also help you demonstrate your attentiveness. When we're communicating on video calls, it's all too tempting to multitask and let our eyes stray to all the other urgent or unnecessary items on our desktop crying out for our attention—all the pop-up notifications, social media posts, important email tasks, and so forth. A great way to show your audience you are not distracted is by transparently telling them what your eyes are looking at when they stray around the landscape of your screen. That can sound something like "If you're seeing my eyes roam about, that's because I'm just pulling up the document right now." No one likes to think they're a lower priority than all your other to-do items. Transparency in this context is a great way to show they aren't.

That's an example of what not to hide on virtual calls: Don't hide the fact that your eyes are straying to find something for your audience. But what should you hide? Using the cards; you can take advantage of the Cloak of Invisibility to practice with them imperceptibly. This can take some mindshare, of course, so I recommend using them on low-consequence calls to start.

PRO TIP

The most frequent misstep (no pun intended) people make in the Mistake Is Not a Mistake drill is not giving the mantra or transparency phrase enough weight. Maybe they skip it entirely. Maybe they mutter it under their breath. Maybe they abbreviate it into a tepid "well" or "also." So be a stickler about the phrase, and discipline yourself to use this mantra and transparency phrases with conviction.

By the way, "A Mistake Is Not a Mistake" is a six-word story. Regardless of whether Hemingway was the father of six-word stories, they are a powerful tool to synthesize big ideas in few words. And I want you to practice synthesis right now, because—congratulations!—you have just completed all the skill-building chapters of *Don't Say Um*.

So I want you to write a six-word story about: (1) what you have learned in this book; or (2) what you will do differently because of it. I'll give you a few examples to get the juices flowing:

- This book taught me the "how."
- Use my body more; brain less.
- Stop trying to stop being nervous.

PLEASE WRITE IN YOUR OWN HERE:

_____

_____

_____

I hope that's the first of many six-word stories this book inspires you to write. In fact, if you like what you just wrote, turn it into a mantra. You might even choose to post it somewhere where you see it frequently. Where is such a place? Lots of people I coach use the wallpaper screensaver on their smart device as a kind of recurrent visual cue. That's just one way to keep these skills top of mind.

What are some other ones? That's the subject of Chapter 19. Let's get to building your daily communication regimen.

CHAPTER 19

MAKING IT STICK

Building Your Daily Communication Regimen

You have just achieved a great feat! The skill-building chapters are over. You are armed with new skills for your old problems.

Just like an athlete, a performer, or any person trying to grow, building new skills takes ongoing—often daily—commitment. And so it is with the techniques you have learned in this book; you have to get your reps in! I want to help you build a daily communication regimen.

What is such a regimen? It's simply the way you are going to transform the contents of this book from information on its pages to memory in your muscles.

To do so, I'm going to walk you through a series of questions. If you feel like using your responses to build and then integrate this regimen into your life right now, great. Do so! If you want to read this chapter, ponder its questions, and then create and commit to your regimen later, also great!

But no matter when you do it, make sure you do it.

If you need help, visit dontsayum.com, and we can help you build your own communication regimen.

To the questions...

AREA 1: CHOOSING YOUR SKILLS

I don't recommend working on more than a couple primary skills at once for a few reasons. One, there is a big risk to "keeping everything in mind." If you try to remember everything and keep it all in "the back of your head," you're probably not holding yourself accountable in a specific way to any one thing. Thus, your improvement dies a slow death by a thousand cuts of generality. More importantly, you don't need to focus on everything because the most important skill for you probably unlocks all the others through the Virtuous Cycle of Good Communication. Rely on that cycle. It is powerful.

Also, you can change your skill focus endlessly, so don't feel any pressure to get this "right" from the beginning. In fact, the more "right" you get it, the more it will change as you build new skills and habits and therefore decide to focus on new areas of need. If you develop your *linguistic precision*, for example, you may want to shift to *gestural freedom and ease* next. This can change, and change again and again. But choose a skill that is right for now and commit to it.

Questions in This Area

- What is the most important and transformative tool/skill/exercise/idea that you have learned in this book?
- What is the second most important and transformative tool/skill/exercise/idea that you have learned in this book?
- If there is a third, what is it?
- Of those skills and tools, which do you want to build into your life?

AREA 2: PRACTICE OPPORTUNITIES

When contemplating when and how to practice, it's best to have variety (just like with vocal presence). What you're looking for is a variety of low-, medium-, and high-consequence opportunities; a variety of professional and social situations; a variety of audience size and composition; a variety of perceptible performance activities (practicing with Lego blocks solo) and imperceptible (subtly placing your finger down on your thigh); and so on. Look for variety and be creative.

Questions in This Area

+ How many days per week do you want to commit to developing these skills? (Be ambitious but realistic—I suggest a minimum of three days; five is better; seven is ideal.)
+ On those days, when will you practice solo without an audience?
  * This is the equivalent of doing your scales while learning the piano or your vocab drills when learning a foreign language. Schedule that practice time!
+ What existing opportunities for practice do you already have?
  * These can be obvious such as presentations, conference calls, committee meetings, and PTO events; they can also be less conventional, like ordering coffee, escalating an issue with a customer service agent, or chitchat with strangers in your day-to-day.
+ What are the new opportunities for practice that you can create?
  * Can you generate new places for yourself? For example, can you create some type of opportunity to give a speech? Nerve-racking to consider? Good! That means you should do it!

AREA 3: HOW TO REMEMBER AND REMIND

Make the act of reminding yourself as brainless as possible. Use your big, powerful brain for worthy tasks like synthesis, contemplation, and cognition, not menial ones like to-do list recall. It's best to build your regimen in a way that makes the practice automatic.

Questions in This Area

+ How do you want to remind yourself throughout your day? Here are some of the favorite mnemonic devices and triggers I've suggested clients use:

  * Change the screensaver/wallpaper on your smart device or computer to show a mantra or picture that reminds you of your skill focus.

  * Choose a helper each week who will be your practice target. You can let this person know about their selection, or not (that is, you don't have to tell them). Whenever you see and interact with them, they are your reminder to practice your skill.

  * Set an alarm on your phone to go off at the same time every day and that next segment of time is your practice time. Practice with the person with whom you are interacting (if you're not interacting with anyone at that moment, practice solo).

  * Place sticky-note reminders strategically around your work and home. Inventiveness matters with this. Maybe even find fun, unconventional locations that continually surprise: tucked under the sun visor on the driver's side of your car; inside the medicine cabinet in a bathroom; on top of the alarm clock; inside a clothes closet door; in your wallet next to a most-used credit card or ID; inside the top drawer of your desk; under your standing workstation, affixed to the mechanism that raises or lowers it; others—be creative!

  * Set obnoxiously colored calendar reminders throughout your schedule before communication interactions.

  * Choose physical architecture mnemonics—remind yourself to practice by walking through certain doorways, riding in certain elevators, navigating in certain hallways, discussing in certain rooms or other physical situations.

  * Anchor your practice to some portion of your commute.

For example, lots of my clients do tongue twisters in the car while driving to work or on the street as they walk to their office, school, or organization.

* Create hidden visual prompts, like a small icon or logo on all the slides of a given presentation that is a reminder to you to do your skill. Make it small, unobtrusive, and generic enough that audience members would be none the wiser.

+ What rituals or disciplines do you already have to which you can anchor a communication regimen?

* You might already exercise, meditate, tidy, groom, or some-other-daily-action-verb in a religiously consistent way. You're already doing the heavy lifting in terms of discipline and scheduling, so consider grafting your communication regimen onto that as an additional five to ten minutes. Here's a simple example I mentioned in the "Practice or Performance" section at the end of Chapter 8 (Enunciation): After you brush your teeth each morning, use the head of the toothbrush as an impediment à la the cork drill, and practice that exercise for a few minutes.

+ Who could be your potential human reminder?

* Remember, you are not required to tell them they are your reminder (although you certainly can if you prefer).

+ What architectural reminders could you use?

* Look for the repeated spaces you navigate in your day-to-day.

+ In what part of your commute could you weave in your regimen?

* Remember that smart devices give you camouflage and permission to warm up and/or practice almost anywhere without passersby noticing. Embrace that freedom!

AREA 4: HOW TO HOLD YOURSELF ACCOUNTABLE

In order to keep growing and unlock continual improvement, you have to stay on track and ensure your regimen is working for you. Happily, you can enlist the help of others in this mission! With that in mind, consider the first question in this area.

Questions in This Area

> + Who can be an accountability partner?
>   * You are not the only human who could improve as a communicator. You've nearly finished reading *Don't Say Um*; why not give it to someone else, tell them to read it, and then team up as each other's practice partners? People tend to stick to new habits, commitments, and resolutions if they have a partner to whom they feel accountable. Consider enlisting someone's help in this case too. Not only will you have the benefit of an accountability partner, but you'll also be putting good energy into the world when you launch their journey of communication improvement.
> + How will you know when you've improved?
>   * What is the measuring stick you can use to validate your progress? I suggest making this as specific and behavioral as possible. Remember: General Don't coaching doesn't work. So don't give yourself some vague goal like "feel better" or "communicate effectively." What do you want to change? Do you want to have the ability to slow your pace? To have software accurately understand and transcribe your speech? To unclench your hands and gesture with freedom and ease? To keep your feet anchored when standing and delivering? Choose a specific goal and use the tools in this book and you will see yourself gain more and more skill. If you need help with this—either in measuring your progress or in identifying a specific goal—use the resources at

CHAPTER 19
MAKING IT STICK

dontsayum.com, including the GK Training practice app, which offers objective metrics.

+ What can you do right now to ensure a next step?

  * For most people, the easiest thing is to put a task or appointment into their digital (or paper) calendar. Why not carve out some time right now to practice, and then add it to your calendar or whatever other reminder system you use to organize your life and time?

Speaking of time, we are almost out of it. Your first trip through this book is nearly complete. Though you have almost finished your first, I hope it's not your only trip. Use this book like a cookbook; go back to the recipes you liked. Try them again. Make the same dish multiple times, and like a chef, you will see your communication "meals" get better and better and better.

But before you start flipping back to the recipes and dishes you want to make again, you have to finish the book. Just two lightning-fast chapters left. Let's get to them.

PART FOUR
———
EVERYTHING ELSE

CHAPTER 20

AI AND THE FUTURE OF DELIVERY

The Future is Delivery.

What do I mean by that? As much as delivery matters, it may be about to matter much, much more. Here's why. Generative AI and large language models and the software built on them—ChatGPT and the like—may have brought humanity to a communication precipice. For all human history, if you wanted to have smart stuff to say, you needed to either be a subject matter expert or rely on one. Now, artificial intelligence can search, sift, and synthesize the totality of human understanding and provide smart responses and content on virtually any subject in virtually no time. I recognize that the accuracy and cogency of some of AI's output aren't always stellar. True; yet AI is currently the worst it will ever be. The speed of its improvement is astonishing.

I've coached in US presidential election cycles multiple times; to ensure candidates are as prepared as possible for any and every communication situation (debates, interviews, etc.), campaigns employ a whole team to source and collate massive amounts of material on given subjects. Usually that all gets collected and organized in an absurdly large binder—a cheat resource that gives candidates a snapshot of the issues as well as potential lines of attack on their opponents. I know the people who create these resources. It is painstaking, rigorous work. It takes smart people working many hours with merciless deadlines to create these tools.

Until now, only the very few had these types of resources. Now—thanks to AI—anyone anywhere can access similarly robust content. Imagine all the situations when people try to say smart stuff—interviews, debates, school board meetings, cocktail hours. The situations for which this otherworldly content cheat could be deployed are practically limitless.

Imagine us all wearing tiny earbuds that feed us expert content in real time. Maybe the aids will even be implants inside our brains. Who knows....

If everyone has equal access to accurate and memorable content, what will distinguish you from the countless others who are also saying dazzling ideas? You guessed it: delivery.

The communicator who can say the spoon-fed content from the AI earbud convincingly will be perceived as better. The communicator who says the same stuff as everyone else but with superior delivery will look like the original one, even though the content is similar.

If this sounds fantastical, maybe it is. I am not a futurist and cannot nor would I try to predict where the future of humanity's intersection with technology is headed. But there is a very real possibility that it is no longer sufficient to "know your stuff" because everyone will be able to say that same stuff, whether they know it or not. You will need to be able to say it with conviction, flare, adamance, and gravitas.

As bizarre (and perhaps dystopic) as that vision may sound, let me remind you of how remarkable you are. Humans are incredibly resourceful creatures. I used to think that cockroaches and mosquitoes would inherit the earth long after we are gone; now I'm not so sure. Just when you think humans are up against the evolutionary ropes, we unleash our industrious, limitless imaginations yet again and devise something like gene editing and CRISPR and gain a potentially game-ending (and terrifying) tool to defeat even mosquitoes.

Given that I am not an evolutionary biologist, what the heck is my point? Humans will find a way. And perhaps we will evolve in response to AI too. We must assume that eventually AI will develop a freakish ability to mimic and reflect human behaviors—even in the category of delivery. How will humans respond then? Will we create "tells" that show other humans we are not "deep fakes," perhaps giving clues when on camera that AI doesn't recognize it should mimic? Will we alter our delivery cadence and patterns ever so slightly so that we're all talking with seemingly random inflections, in essence using arbitrary vocal variety to offer a "tell" that we're human? Or perhaps being in person and giving rousing, in-the-flesh oratory will be the only trusted communication currency, given that anything on camera will be prey to deep fakes?

Who knows. I don't know the future; I do know a smart investment you can make in your own future though: delivery. And speaking of you...the final chapter is all about you.

It's only two hundred four words, and it's intended as inspiration, not instruction. Turn the page when you're ready.

CHAPTER 21

LAST CHAPTER

n the introduction I shared this three-part statement:

**COMMUNICATION MATTERS,
IT'S MORE PHYSICAL THAN YOU THINK,
AND THERE ARE THINGS YOU CAN DO
TO IMPROVE IT.**

Hopefully, you recognize now that all three portions are true. But the final thought I want to offer you in *Don't Say Um* is different: *communicators* matter. And we need honorable, moral communicators! We live in a dynamic time, both exciting and fraught. There are more ways than ever to communicate and more people than ever on the planet communicating—7.8 billion potential communicators, in fact (and still growing). Some of those are communicating wonderful messages; some aren't.

In my line of work, you very frequently encounter incredible communicators who are not incredible people. You know who tend to be great at presenting, but not so great for the planet? Narcissists and egomaniacs. I steer clear of coaching those folks when I meet them.

But the world can't rid itself of good communicators saying bad things for bad purposes. I have seen, over the decades, that very often the people with the best ideas aren't necessarily speaking with the loudest voices.

You have something to say. Use this book to learn how to say it clearly, powerfully, persuasively. The world needs you.

ACKNOWLEDGMENTS

To my collaborator, composer, partner, editor, brainstormer, fellow dreamer, and...oh yeah...wife, Hilary Kole, thank you immeasurably for so many things but most of all for eternally having my back. Beans, baby.

To the GK Training crew who helped *Don't Say Um* along this journey: Dana Altier-Jeske, Ben Graney, Shawn Fagan, Cassandra Freeman, Sarah Kinsey, Joe Varca. You are the greatest team a CEO could ask for. Thank you! The best is yet to come....

To my agent, Byrd Leavell, at UTA, thanks for your camaraderie and support and for instantly recognizing that this book isn't about public speaking but rather living. And to Dan Milaschewski at UTA, thanks for your infectious enthusiasm, your spirit of giving, and your sheer intellect. Your clients and clients-to-be are fortunate.

To Dan Ambrosio at Hachette Go, thanks for your invaluable input, your vision, and for using the GK Lego drill in your initial pitch meeting at Hachette (!).

To Hachette production editor Sean Moreau, copy editor Christina Palaia, and proofreaders Martha Knauf and Lori Lewis, thank you for giving *Don't Say Um* its final meticulous review.

To my family—Jeff, Dan, Kim, Dave, Krista (and all the second generations after them)—thank you for always being there for me.

To my mom, thank you for teaching me perseverance.

To my dad (posthumously), thank you for teaching me how to take risks.

To the acting teachers I have known and learned from at every level of my education: Jim Malcolm, Gary Logan, Andrew Wade, Deb Hecht, Ron Van Lieu, Janet Zarish, Jim Calder, Bev Wideman, Shane Ann Younts, David Hammonds, Ralph Zito, Daniel Pardo, Gwen Ellison, Shari Van Haselen, and more. Thank you for everything you have taught me but most of all thank you for dedicating your lives to the worthiest of purposes—helping workaday human beings accomplish the magical, sacred act of creating art from nothing but our bodies and breath. I appreciate you so very much.

To Andrew Yang, thank you for your courage and fearless drive to do the next right thing. You inspire me.

To my mentor, Neal Baer, thank you for your generosity and your brilliance. The world is lucky to have you.

To Nicola Kraus, thanks for being a force for momentum and action when this project needed it most.

Last, if I could thank every person I have ever coached, I would list each of you here by name. The lessons of dedication, grit, openness, bravery, logic, perseverance, and risk I have gained from you live with me every day. Thank you for your trust, belief, and will to improve.